The Collected Works of Edith Stein

X

The Collected Works of

EDITH STEIN

Sister Teresa Benedicta of the Cross
Discalced Carmelite

1891 - 1942

Volume Ten

ICS Publications
Institute of Carmelite Studies
Washington, D.C.

2006

EDITH STEIN

Sister Teresa Benedicta of the Cross
Discalced Carmelite

An Investigation Concerning the State

Edited and translated by Marianne Sawicki

ICS Publications
Institute of Carmelite Studies
Washington, D.C.
2006

Library of Congress Cataloging-in-Publication Data

Stein, Edith, Saint, 1891-1942.
    [Eine Untersuchung über den Staat. English]
    An investigation concerning the state / Edith Stein ;
edited and translated by Marianne Sawicki.
        p. cm. – (Collected works of Edith Stein ; v. 10)
    Includes bibliographical references and index.
    ISBN 0-935216-39-1
    1. Psychology and philosophy. 2. Phenomenological
    psychology. 3. Social psychology. 4. State, The.
    I. Sawicki, Marianne. II. Title. III. Series: Stein, Edith,
    Saint, 1891-1942. Works. English. 1986 ; v. 10.
B3332.S672 E54 1986 vol. 10
[BF41]
193 s--dc22
[320.1]
                                  2005023852

Contents

Preface to the ICS Publications Edition

This tenth volume in the ICS Publications edition of The Collected Works of Edith Stein reveals a side of the author less familiar to most readers, particularly those in the English-speaking world. Though relatively brief, *An Investigation Concerning the State* is Stein's most sustained contribution to political philosophy, and therefore an important text for appreciating her multifaceted life and interests. Here she attempts to clarify such major theoretical issues as the nature of the nation-state itself as human and political entity, its proper autonomy and power, the significance of human rights, guilt, and punishment, and the role of law, ethics, and religion in relation to the state.

As a philosophical study, this text builds organically upon her earlier investigations of the human person and community, as found especially in her doctoral dissertation, *The Problem of Empathy,* and in her *Philosophy of Psychology and the Humanities.* But for Edith Stein the concerns addressed herein are not merely theoretical. Throughout her life she maintained a strong interest and involvement in the pressing social and political issues of her time. Describing her days at university in *Life in a Jewish Family,* she speaks of her "passionate participation in current political events as history in the making" and her "extraordinarily strong social conscience, a feeling for the solidarity not only of all mankind but also of smaller social entities" (p. 190). Early on, she joined the struggle for women's suffrage in Germany, and after her conversion to Christianity became a leading voice in the Catholic women's movement in German-speaking Europe. Later still, in 1933, she had someone hand-deliver a letter of protest against the Nazi "campaign of extermination against Jewish blood" to Pope Pius XI appealing for his intervention and warning that the responsibility for the sad consequences of Nazi abuses "must fall, after all, on those who brought them to this point and...those who keep silent in the face of such happenings."

Ultimately she was arrested and sent to Auschwitz as part of swift official reprisals against the Dutch Catholic bishops for speaking out against Nazi anti-Jewish policies. Thus she died at the hands of a state that countervened nearly every principle she had outlined in the present treatise. Declaring her co-patron of Europe in 1999, Pope John Paul II remarked that her witness stands as "a protest against every violation of the fundamental rights of the human person" and as a sign of the need "to form a truly fraternal society."

ICS Publications welcomes the opportunity to publish *An Investigation Concerning the State* for the first time in English, and is grateful to to Marianne Sawicki, the translator and editor of our edition, for her generous dedication to this project even in very difficult times. By rendering Stein's often dense German philosophical prose into idiomatic English, and by providing ample explanatory notes, she has made this important text far more accessible. May its readers be inspired also to work toward that world of justice and peace for which Edith Stein and so many others gave their lives.

Steven Payne, OCD
Series Editor of The Collected Works of Edith Stein

Editor's Introduction

This treatise on politics was utterly ignored when first published in 1925. One searches in vain for citations or criticisms of it in the scholarly literature of that day. Even its author had moved on to other interests by the time the treatise appeared in print, never to refer to it again[1]. Yet readers today take up this work in hopes of finding a missing link, a key to a puzzle. In fact, Edith Stein's *Investigation Concerning the State* fits into an unusually wide range of contexts, none of which could have been perceived in 1925.

Today we can begin to say what this work means. Today we know that Germany in 1925 was soon to enter the era of National Socialism, the Second World War, and the Holocaust. Today we know that Edith Stein completed this treatise on the very brink of a religious conversion that would carry her heart to Carmel, her mind to Aquinas and John of the Cross, her body to Auschwitz, and her name to the roster of canonized saints in the Catholic Church.

Stein today is venerated as a martyr of church-state conflict and as a heavenly patroness of Europe. But this treatise is quite earthly. This is no mystical revelation; it is a tough-minded and tightly reasoned philosophical essay, relentlessly driving the reader through a series of arguments. Stein's trademark, as a philosopher, was to demand that her students and readers follow her reasoning by re-enacting all the steps, and in this way come to see for themselves the necessity of the conclusions.

---

1. A footnote in *Finite and Eternal Being* (CWES 9: 602) mentioning this treatise was likely inserted by the editor of the 1950 German edition.

This demand presupposes a certain facility with the techniques and the terminology of "phenomenology," which is the tradition of philosophical analysis in which Stein worked. Here is perhaps the greatest challenge for today's reader. As a young woman, Stein practiced a form of phenomenology that she had learned from her teacher Edmund Husserl *before* he developed the "transcendental phenomenology" that is better known today, and also *before* the turn to "existentialism" inaugurated by Martin Heidegger, which so decisively shaped the agenda of European philosophy in the twentieth century. To understand Stein, one must take care not to read back into her work the premises of existentialism or of transcendental phenomenology—much less those of her own later writings. At the same time, one must bear in mind the premises and vocabulary commonly accepted by phenomenologists working in 1925. In other words, Stein deserves to be read in precisely her own intellectual context.

That's where the editor's footnotes come in. Comments marked off by brackets [like this] provide information that would have been taken for granted by Stein's original philosophical readers. In addition, some editorial footnotes supply background for certain religious questions that may occur. No reader will need *all* the footnotes, of course; but they are offered in the hope that no reader will turn away in discouragement from the challenge of following Stein's thought.

1. PLAN OF THE TREATISE. What are states, and why do we have them? The two parts of the volume address the two halves of this deceptively simple question. The answer is equally simple. States are agencies for making and enforcing laws. We have them not by necessity, not for their own sakes, but merely to accomplish various functions that benefit human beings. This is easy to say, but difficult to demonstrate. The question must be broken down into its components and carefully examined.

Part I, the bulk of the work, presents an eidetic analysis of the state. Phenomenology examines the *eidos* or "essence" of something, apart from whether it actually exists and apart from the conditions that may accompany and affect it during its historical existence. The essence of the state eludes those who seek it in some primordial contract, for many states have come into being through conquest and not through any voluntary deal-making.

The essence of the state pertains to all states, no matter how they originated, and so it must be sought apart from history. Stein submits the state to eidetic analysis in three stages, corresponding to the three sections of part I. First, the state is considered as one kind of social group among others, and specifically one kind of community among other communities, with which it may share members. Distinctions are drawn between the state and the nation or ethnic group, and between the state and its territory.[2]

Second, the state is considered, somewhat paradoxically, as both the maker of laws and subjected to law. This requires a distinction that is difficult to express, both in German and in English. German *Recht* can mean either "law" or "right." Before any civil law was ever enacted or placed on the books, "right and wrong" already were operative. The phenomenological term for this pre-existing absolute relationship is "pure law." This is what obliges states, as they go about their task of making and enforcing particular laws. While "pure law" does not require states to be, there is only one way for them to come into existence and maintain themselves: by self-assertion. A state must be sovereign; and if sovereignty is lost, there is no longer a state. Yet sovereignty is possible in many forms. The third section examines factors that, in principle,

---

2. Obviously, Maryland and California would not be states in this sense, since a federal government exercises power over them. The "United States" is one state, in Stein's sense.

would determine what sort of state would emerge in a given situation. Although concrete examples are cited, these are only for illustration. The analysis is still eidetic and *a priori*. Throughout Part I the focus remains on possibility, prior to any historical experience.

Part II brings the discussion into the realm of historical process. Stein grapples here with the leading theories of German Idealism, which now are revealed as the opponent that she had in view all along. Philosophers like Immanuel Kant, G.W.F. Hegel, and J.G. Fichte regarded the state as a factor necessarily emerging in a grand historical process, whether as an end in itself or as one phase destined to be superceded by another. Stein demonstrates that any such conception is untenable. States, she argues, can be neither explained nor justified by citing random historical causes or by projecting fanciful teleologies. Their true being is to implement law, whose source subsists quite independently.

Although Part II is the shorter, it consists of six sections. These attempt to identify grounds for assessing the value and legitimacy of the various kinds of states and state agencies, and of the state as such. Careful consideration of the standard theories leads repeatedly to findings that state values are secondary and derivative. Value accrues primarily to personal and community characteristics such as liberty, conscience, cultural creativity, and religious conviction. The state puts itself at risk whenever it goes up against those.

2. PLACE WITHIN STEIN'S PHILOSOPHY. Stein began work on her treatise *Concerning the State* some time before October 1920. The manuscript was completed by the end of the next summer, when it was given to a friend to read, and by October of 1922 the work was being prepared for press. These dates are known from the few mentions of the work in Stein's correspondence.

The letters also suggest a reason why Stein took up this

topic. An armistice had ended the First World War on 11 November 1918, but Germany had already entered a period of increasing domestic instability. After the collapse of the imperial government in the revolution of November 1918, Stein returned to her mother's home in Breslau and immediately immersed herself in political affairs. She joined the German Democratic Party and, as she wrote to her friend Roman Ingarden on 30 November 1918, she anticipated being appointed to its executive committee. During the following weeks, Stein wrote to Ingarden of feverish political activity: organizing the youth, building coalitions with other leaders, and hammering out positions on issues such as women's suffrage.

Yet she soon tired of this activism, and on 27 December 1918, told Ingarden that she was sick of politics. "I totally lack what it takes: a tough conscience and a thick hide," she wrote. "I feel completely uprooted and homeless among the people I've got to deal with." Nevertheless, she said, she would have to hang on until the election of the National Assembly, which took place on 19 January 1919. Delegates elected on that day would meet to frame the constitution for the German Republic—known to history as the Weimar Republic—which was adopted on 11 August 1919. The new government was doomed from the start because of the severe terms imposed upon Germany as reparations by the victors at the Treaty of Versailles. The new year 1920 brought ruinous economic depression to the country, aggravating the post-war political instability. The infant democracy had to fight for its life both at home and in international affairs.

Practical problems of everyday survival were interlaced with theoretical issues that piqued Stein's philosophical interest. It appears that she rebounded from her brief foray into activism and returned to the more congenial tasks of research. Yet grass-roots politics can be profoundly influenced, for good or ill, by ideas and ideologies lying unexamined beneath the discourse and decisions of the day. Stein expresses concern, toward the end of Part I of this work, that a perverse theory of the state has the potential for eroding civic life. Thus in the treatise *Concerning the State*, she undertakes to construct a wholesome basic theory to be offered as an antidote to the ideologies then in abundant supply in Germany.[3]

Stein's text indicates that she consulted the standard textbooks of constitutional law and political history, areas in which she had trained during her university studies with Max Lehmann in 1913-1915. Yet her guiding questions now stem from phenomenology. In particular, she builds upon the analyses of the foundations of law worked out by another of her teachers, Adolf Reinach, along with her own earlier work on the social connections obtaining among human beings.

That work sets the stage for this. The treatise *Concerning the State* is the last of Stein's four phenomenological treatises. The first was her dissertation *On the Problem of Empathy* (CWES 1), written for Edmund Husserl and published in 1917. It establishes that someone's experiences are accessible to others under certain very specific conditions. Experiences flow along in a way that is described as "motivated." One understands the experience of another by feeling the tug of the successive motivations that originally propelled that experience along, and thus also feeling the non-necessary choices among motivations that the originating person made. Experiences of several sorts are selectively open to be followed by other human beings in this way; for example, in narratives, in proofs, in arguments, in decisions, in actions. The German term *Einfühlung,* literally "in-feeling" or "feeling-into," covers

---

3. The year of its publication, 1925, also saw the appearance of Adolf Hitler's programmatic *Mein Kampf,* the bible of National Socialism, which addresses many of the same questions that Stein examines here. A comparison of the two reveals them as diametrically opposed responses to the same urgent situation.

all of those instances. Although this term is translated "empathy," it does not primarily denote an emotional sharing. What is shared is content, which is re-lived in whatever way is appropriate to it.

"Motivation" in phenomenology is one of two contrasting principles that account for the forward flow of events in time, the other being "causality." Motivation is detected by being inwardly felt, as an urge that is resistible and therefore noncausal. Causality is detected by being opaque to inward feeling; for causes affect us externally and involuntarily, not by appealing to our free choice. Real life events thus always involve an interplay of motivation and causality, that is, of free choice and unfree reaction. To understand the world around us, we use empathy to sort out what "merely happened" from what was deliberate and meaningful.

Human behavior, too, seems to be a mixture of caused and chosen events. In Stein's day, the young science of psychology was searching for a method to make sense of human behavior. Some theorists wanted to limit psychology to causal explanations. Stein's second phenomenological treatise, "Sentient Causality" (CWES 7: 2-128), recommended an alternative approach. The natural world, she argued, is understood to be a closed system completely governed by relations of causality. Energy is conserved within that system. But human behavior does not obey the laws of the conservation of energy, and therefore cannot be accounted for in terms of causality alone. In a human organism, transformations of energy occur through nutrition and metabolism, exercise and rest. But the output of work cannot be predicted on the basis of physically available energy. Stein pointed to a number of instances where the potential for work is either enhanced or diminished through infusions of meaning. Conversely, the making of meaning can effectively multiply the potential for work many times beyond the level predictable on the basis of energy input to the system physically. Sentience, then, comprises an interface between the worlds of matter and of value.

Along with this non-closure of the human organism with respect to the causally determined world, Stein also established the non-closure of the human individual, so-called, with respect to other human beings. She described phenomena in which energy, the ability to do work, is transmitted among individuals through meaning. The third of her phenomenological treatises, "Individual and Community" (CWES 7: 129-314), explored the role of communities as power reservoirs in the circuits of potent meanings that link and empower individuals. Many of the examples discussed in that treatise had to do with the affairs of nations, governments, and ethnic groups, all of which exemplify phenomena of community. Stein also discussed the place of the individual as a conduit for the transfer of energy and meaning among the various communities to which one might belong: family, workplace, friends, political party, intellectual circle, nation.

One persistent theme was the issue of how an individual may join or may leave a community, and what consequences may follow for the life and work of either. While not overtly autobiographical, those discussions certainly reflect Stein's personal experience of conflicting allegiances. During her lifetime she revered the university as an institution, yet struggled to change its policies and practices. She was a loyal subject of the Prussian monarch, Kaiser Wilhelm II, yet joined the German Democratic Party. She cherished her large Jewish family, yet was contemplating Christian baptism by the time she completed this, the fourth and last of her phenomenological treatises, *An Investigation Concerning the State.*

Readers today approach this text with various questions. Does it perhaps offer a clue to Stein's religious conversion, which immediately followed the writing of this treatise? There is a hint of this in the excursus on guilt which interrupts Part II of the work. In that passage, Stein criticizes another writer's attempt to reason to the existence of God through a phenomenology of punishment. In her estimation, that particular attempt fails, for technical reasons.

Yet the goal of achieving phenomenological insight into the divine reality seems first to have occurred to Stein just here. She would go on to pursue this goal in her mature work—starting not with punishment and justice, but with temporality and desire (CWES 9). Stein wrote to Ingarden on 30 August 1921, that the completed manuscript *Concerning the State* had been left behind at a friend's house: "I've now begun an article on philosophy of religion here at home. What will become of it, I don't yet know. But in future I'll probably work only in that field." This prediction turned out to be true.

The treatise *Concerning the State* is therefore something of a dead end in the development of Stein's social theory. It expanded and applied the constructive work of the three earlier treatises, but it bore no fruit in its own day. Stein herself turned away from political theory, as she had earlier abandoned political activism, and looked elsewhere to find the sources that would nourish her own life and thought. By the late 1920s, a mood of nationalism and anti-intellectualism was overtaking political and social discourse throughout Germany.

3. ISSUES. Yet arguments are neither defeated nor destroyed by being ignored. As a phenomenologist, Stein argues from logical necessity, not from historical happenstance. This means that the work has validity independent of the particular circumstances in which it was written. Here is one of the ways in which its martyred author survives the Holocaust, in the course of which she was murdered by the German state. "Martyr" means "witness." This treatise testifies against state power gone mad. It rewards careful reading today, for at many points it is stunningly relevant to issues arising in our own era of economic globalization, ethnic cleansing, and wars for regime change.

Moreover, certain components of Stein's philosophical anthropology undergo significant development in this treatise, including the technical concepts soul, person, and freedom. Other concepts explored here would become distorted features of the hateful rhetoric of National Socialism: race, land, nation.

On questions of jurisprudence, government, and constitutional law, Stein the phenomenologist confronts and challenges the major theoretical options of her day: natural law theory, the legal positivism of the Vienna circle, and the neo-Kantian "pure theory of law" propounded by Hans Kelsen.[4] Stein argues instead for a theory of "pure law." That is, she insists that right and wrong are realities understood to be independent of the mind that knows them yet accessible to it, while at the same time she denies that right and wrong are features of "nature," naively construed.

A sampling of the key issues examined within this treatise may provide a helpful overview.

Law. The state is essentially bound up with the making and enforcing of law, yet it is not the originator of rightness and wrongness as such. The relational nexus of claims and obligations, contracts and compliance, is already *there* before

---

4. Stein does not cite him by name. Kelsen, professor at the University of Vienna and later at Cologne, developed his "pure theory of law" in several scholarly articles and books during the late 1910s and 1920s. It became a touchstone of twentieth century legal theory, and was summed up in a 1934 treatise that was widely read and translated. See Hans Kelsen, *Introduction to the Problems of Legal Theory,* trans. Bonnie Litschewski Paulson and Stanley L. Paulson (Oxford: Clarendon Press, 1992). Like Stein, Kelsen was dismissed from his teaching position in April 1933 by the Nazi regime. Unlike Stein, he left Germany with his family and resumed his career in America.

the state comes on the scene. This "pure law" or "pure right" is merely instantiated, more or less adequately, in those statutes and regulations that states may happen to enact. Here we see how staunch a realist Stein is in the practice of phenomenology. As she builds her arguments, the network of right relations does not need to be ordained by God, much less evolved by human cultural practices or devised through political deal-making. It *simply obtains*. And it presents itself to the human mind, in insight, without needing to be mediated either through observation of real-world events, or through deductive reasoning from principles, or through authoritative divine revelation. This adamantly realist stance may confound readers who are more accustomed to cultural relativism and social constructivism. It may shock those who expect theological solutions to secular dilemmas. Be forewarned: no orthodoxy escapes the scalpel of this ruthlessly honest thinker.

Political science.   Stein presumes that readers are as familiar as she is with the tenets of German Idealism regarding history and the role of the state in it. She undertakes to demolish the commonly held belief that history consists in the progressive and inevitable self-expression of rationality. She argues against both Hegel's view of the necessity of the state, and Fichte's and Marx's views on the necessary disappearance of the state. All such theories go wide of reality, since they project essential structures on the basis of mere historical events, which in principle cannot be known in their entirety. Stein instead uses phenomenology's "eidetic" analysis to prune back the overgrowth of Idealist theories and get at the underlying "fabric" (*Struktur*) of political life. The *science* of political science—that is, its systematic method of inquiring into civic affairs, reaching conclusions, and predicting events—is not properly a political affair itself; and so its foundation must be secured through logical and phenomenological means. (The same goes for any empirical science.)

Were political science to be left to bootstrap itself through its own empirical methods of observation and generalization, it would degenerate into rhetoric and would cease to be science. While it might retain considerable power to *persuade,* its results could not be certified as true and reliable. In phenomenology, the term "investigation" (*Untersuchung*) signifies the work of providing reliable foundations for empirical science; hence the title which Stein gave to this treatise.

Person and personality. The term "person" has a technical meaning and is always used with precision by Stein. Even though the meaning of this term underwent some development for Stein between 1917 and the early 1930s, it is never a synonym for human individual. It names that aspect of rational individuals and communities that carries unique value and is capable of creative expression. For example, a human individual exhibits various phenomenal regions characterized by different sorts of receptivity and closure with respect to other regions. The physical body is open to influences from the physical world, and also harbors a sentient region that is open to the sentience of other human and animal organisms. This sentience in turn is open to a region of mental phenomena, also shareable with other minds. Those modes of openness account for energy transfer within and among individuals.

But next to all that, there is the realm of the personal. It gives access to the realm of value, but does *not* open directly to other persons. Interpersonal contact is instead mediated through mind and sentience. *That which* is mediated in this way may include the person's unique "take" on values, that is, those aspects of value that are uniquely available to the person she is.[5] Strictly speaking there are no human "individuals" as

---

5. The noun *Person* in German is feminine in its grammatical gender. Although the sense is inclusive, Stein sometimes plays the corresponding feminine pronouns off against those for

such, because of this constitutive openness and connection. Humanity is community. Particular communities, too, exhibit this region of phenomena characterized as personal. They have *Personalität* or *Persönlichkeit*, terms which Stein uses interchangeably. For example, each ethnic group taps into value as no other group can. It mediates this access in its creative cultural achievements, thus rendering the unique values accessible to the minds and feelings of others. Stein insists that there is ultimately one overarching community, that is, the commonality of rational minds, insuring the possibility of communication of values among all peoples.

The state is not a person, for it has no such access to value. It relies instead on communities for its value, particularly the nation or the ethnic communities of which it may be comprised. This must be noted because the term "juridical person" crops up in legal jargon. Such a legal entity is not really a person, in the sense that Stein confers upon the term.

Besides having access to unique value, the person is uniquely the source of free and creative choices. This goes for human individuals and communities alike. Only persons initiate actions; and when a state is said to act, this means only that persons who are vested with proper authority have acted on behalf of the state. Therefore the persons always bear responsibility for their actions; they cannot abdicate it by transferring it to the state, nor can the state demand absolute obedience from its representatives or its citizens. Yet the state requires continuing recognition from persons, or else it dissolves.

Soul and spirit. The term *Seele* and adjectives related to it present special problems in translation. In English, "soul" ordinarily suggests a religious context, and hardly ever is it

---

Individuum, which are neuter, and those for *Mensch,* which are masculine.

used adjectivally. In German, *Seele* has a broader range of meaning, which includes everyday secular experiences as well as religious ones. The adjective *seelisch* can appear where Americans might say mental, spiritual, psychological, emotional, or heartfelt. In Stein's early phenomenology, "soul" is not a religious term. It refers to literary and artistic sensibilities, especially those associated with German cultural values. The younger Stein never describes a human being as composed of "body and soul," but rather as exhibiting the four phenomenal regions mentioned above: the physical, the sentient, the mental, and the personal. Strictly speaking, *all* of those are located in the body, and all are equally soulful.

How is this phenomenological anthropology, already well thought out and presented in the earlier treatises, to be reconciled with the classical "body and soul" anthropology that Stein would encounter in Christian writers after her religious conversion? This problem would be addressed by Stein in the early 1930s in *Potency and Act,* a forthcoming volume in this series. The solution is not yet in sight in the present treatise *Concerning the State,* although Stein begins to address some religious questions with due seriousness. The term "soul" now covers phenomena and functions that previously had been parceled out into separate discussions of empathy, sentience, mind, and community. In lieu of a definition of soul, Stein asserts that three kinds of experiences register in this realm of human being:

1. the person's attitudes or stances, along with the ability to take a stand at all on matters of value and truth;

2. the person's inner links to other persons, along with the capacity for entering into such intimacy at all; and

3. the person's own unique creations in art, craft, or science, along with the very possibility of creating new works of beauty and new ways of knowing reality.

Thus the soul is characterized by its openness; it is not yet imagined to be an interior castle with portals to lock down. The term will become increasingly important for Stein from this point on, signaling a certain shift in the direction of her philosophical development. Yet in this treatise its meaning is still not primarily religious, for the soul is treated as *the* medium of *all* interpersonal access.

Therefore, the reader is warned that Stein's theorization of the soul is a work in progress. The same caveat applies to the term *Geist,* which means mind or mentality or spirit. In German this term does not sound especially religious or mystical. In the present treatise, it is used for the most part in a non-religious sense. But editorial footnotes alert the reader to the use of the terms *Geist* and *Seele* and their cognates wherever there is a possibility of ambiguous meaning.

Race and land. Perhaps no other concept is more fraught with political controversy than these two. In Stein's day, they were becoming the keystone of National Socialist ideology. In our day, they still remain flash points for ethnic conflicts on all continents, including North America. Stein regards different races of human beings as different repertoires of adaptation to the distinctive opportunities, inspirations, and challenges presented by different landscapes. Races and ethnic groups are significant as culturally creative entities. That means that they perceive and actualize unique values, making those values available to other races and ethnic groups. Thus for Stein, race is a principle of cultural productivity and of openness among human beings, not of separation or alienation. The universal human capacity for empathy ensures that this will be so. Stein's view contrasts sharply with Nazi racial doctrine, according to which the possibility of empathy and cultural understanding is restricted to those who share racial identity, and race itself is limited to physical inherited traits.

War and armed conflicts. Given Stein's well known patriotism and her wholehearted support for her country during the First World War, it is not surprising to find that in this treatise she endorses the necessity of armed forces. The state must have the means to enforce the laws and suppress rebellion on the domestic front, just as it must have the means to prevent other states from imposing coercive measures from afar. In cases where citizens may wish to withdraw their recognition from the state, Stein even foresees the use of force to persuade them otherwise. Yet curiously, these arguments in favor of armed force are mitigated by a critique of coercion that appears toward the end of the treatise (in Part II §4.b.). Stein writes that a conflict of values can never be settled through external conflict. It must be resolved inwardly by each person. She asserts that the state is not permitted to disregard any values, not even those of its enemies. The fact that states, or their representatives, often prove to be incapable of grasping the values of the opposing side is what leads to armed conflicts, but the fact of war also demonstrates that the decisions preceding it, whatever they might have been, were wrong.

Religion. Conflict among values is the context in which Stein takes up the issue of religion, almost as an afterthought. The present treatise offers no statement of Stein's own belief; it merely compares hypothetical positions. The theory of divine sovereignty, proposed by Christian believers, conflicts with the idea of state sovereignty, Stein remarks. On one hand, the theory of divine sovereignty implies that *all* existing states, and not just theocracies so-called, in fact exist only because the deity wills them to be. There's nothing in the idea of the state to render it incompatible with divine governance of the world; having a God does not rule out having such things as states. On the other hand, the state must be sovereign over every society within it, including the church. Which view takes precedence? There appears to be a logical standoff.

Stein concludes that this conflict cannot be resolved in principle, but only practically on a case by case basis. Practically speaking, it is imprudent for a state to interfere too severely in religious affairs. This is so because people do in fact have strongly felt religious convictions. If the state imposes regulations that conflict with religious duties, then people are likely to resolve the conflict in favor of religion and against the state, leading to insurrection. Therefore it is wise for the state to refrain from getting itself into such a situation. Moreover, there is an ethical duty to honor the value of religious convictions, regardless of whether those convictions involve mistakes about what exists in reality. The state may not coerce persons to act against their religious beliefs. But it may undertake to dispel their illusions and delusions, and it can provide opportunities for religious education.

4. ACKNOWLEDGMENTS. The work of this translation was supported in part by a Faculty Research Grant from Morgan State University for the summer of 2002, which is gratefully acknowledged. Also of considerable assistance was the orientation to political theory gained during a fellowship year at the Erasmus Institute at the University of Notre Dame, 1998-99. Librarians at the Library of Congress facilitated access to nearly all of the editions of works cited by Stein in this treatise, and Andrew M. Dudash of the L.A. Beeghly Library at Juniata College generously assisted by locating contemporary sources. The translator was fortunate to have at her disposal a set of detailed notes prepared by Walter Redmond, as well as the excellent doctoral dissertations of Sarah Borden and Sister M. Regina van den Berg, O.S.F. Conversations with those scholars also were helpful in the preparation of this work. A debt of gratitude is owed to Sister Josephine Koeppel, OCD, who gave excellent advice and provided access to her research materials. Thanks especially to two

philosophical colleagues: Mette Lebech of the Faculty of Philosophy of the National University of Ireland, Maynooth, whose many substantive comments have vastly improved the translation and the notes, and Father Steven Payne, OCD, who pointed out important historical parallels and, in his role as editor of this series, lent unfailing personal support and professional expertise to bring the project to completion.

This edition appears in advance of the corresponding critical edition soon to be published in the German series Edith Stein Gesamtausgabe—just as happened with volume 7 of the Collected Works of Edith Stein, *Philosophy of Psychology and the Humanities*. Both English and German editions are based directly on the original publications from the 1920s, which were proof-read and corrected before printing by Edith Stein herself. The original manuscripts were not saved.

Stein's German academic diction is complex. Rendering it into viable English involved breaking down the long sentences and paragraphs into more manageable units. In many places, antecedent nouns had to be supplied where pronouns appear in the original. To make Stein's arguments more accessible for today's readers, contractions are sometimes used, and formal third-person idioms are replaced with informal second-person expressions. (The formal expression "one thinks" becomes "you'd think" in idiomatic English.) Stein's numerous uses of hypothetical cases are flagged by the phrase "suppose that . . . ," although this is unnecessary in German and does not appear in the original.

By the grace of God, may the genius of Stein's thought in this treatise reach out to ease the conflicts of our times, notwithstanding the shortcomings of the translation.

MARIANNE SAWICKI

Juniata College
July 2005

Dedicated to Hans Theodor Conrad[1]

I. The ontic fabric of the state[2]

§1. The civil community

The state is a mode of society. This is the [common] starting point for quite divergent theories of the state. Actually, the fact that subjects live in a state, and have rather specific functions in its composition, will turn out to be an indispensable element in the fabric of the state. Hence if we want to get a close look at this fabric, one possible way of going about it is to begin by investigating the modes of living together that are possible in principle for subjects in the state. It remains to be seen whether in this way we can arrive at an exhaustive characterization of what the state is as such. That should in no way be presupposed.

---

1. [Theodor Conrad was a friend and colleague of Edith Stein. His wife was Hedwig Conrad-Martius, a confidante of Stein's who would become Stein's baptismal sponsor. The Conrads extended hospitality to a number of young phenomenologists at their home and apple orchard in the village of Bergzabern. When Stein went to stay with the Conrads in the summer of 1921, she brought along the just-completed manuscript of *An Investigation Concerning the State* for comment.]

2. [*Ontische Struktur*, "ontic fabric," refers to the essence of state as such. This chapter aims to identify the components that are necessary if an entity is to be a state at all. Here there is less concern with the actual institutions that may belong to this or that historical state. According to this way of thinking, any such historically existing institutions are possible for the state because of its ontic fabric.]

I

a) The state as a social pattern;
its relation to crowd, community, and association

In an earlier publication[3] I undertook to work out the types of living together that are possible for subjects.[4] So I can pick up here where I left off, using the results obtained there. I designated the lowest social type as a *mass*.[5] It is characteristic of the mass, I found, that the individuals belonging to it are reciprocally influencing one another without knowing anything about the influence that they exert or receive. Although their behavior may be *similar* because of the reciprocal influence, they don't experience it as *common*. The mass lasts only for as long as the individuals constituting it are in active contact; and it falls apart as soon as that contact breaks off. There's no organization here that outlasts this being-together, nor does any mode of being-together develop objectively apart from the individuals.

We do find such objective modes—civil institutions, in the broadest sense—wherever we are talking about states. And inasmuch as these are indicated by the fabric of a state, as at least possible in principle if not as necessary, the mass cannot be the typical mode of living together in the state. Of course this is not to deny that the individuals within a state often are found together in masses, or that this can become decisively significant for its

---

3. See *Philosophy of Psychology and the Humanities* [volume 7 of The Collected Works of Edith Stein (Washington: ICS Publications, 2000)], second treatise, "Individual and Community" [pages 129-314. It was first published in 1922 in volume 5 of Husserl's *Jahrbuch*. The *Jahrbuch* also published the present treatise in 1925 as part of volume 7.]

4. [*Subjekte*, "subjects," is used here and above in a technical sense to refer to beings who are conscious, rational, and freely active. Only such beings could belong to a state.]

5. [*Masse*, "mass," can also be translated as "crowd" or "mob." "Crowd theory" was described by Gustave LeBon in works that were quite influential in their day. See Stein's critique of "mass contagion" in CWES 7:241-55.]

actual formation. [But] there's no way to get at the fabric of the state as such from that side.

Yet it's feasible to approach this fabric from another angle. We customarily talk about the state as a person.[6] That seems to indicate that we have to look for its place in the realm of mind.[7] Yet we have been unable to detect any mental functioning in the structure of the mass. On the contrary, we found *community* [to be] grounded specifically in what is mental and [to be] marked by the very thing that's missing from the mass: the individuals are living in their common mutuality, "with one another" in a strict sense. Unlike individuals living in the mass, no one goes off into his or her own [private] experiencing. Rather, each has the others given together as accompanying him in his living; each feels herself as a member of the community that, for its part, is subject of a life of its own.[8]

In the life of the community, stable usages build up whose fulfillment can be taken over by different individuals in succes-

---

6. [This usage is found in works on political theory. *Person* for Edith Stein is a technical term and is used with great precision. It is not merely a synonym for "individual" or "human being." A person has an intricate ontic fabric, which Stein has examined in *Philosophy of Psychology*, CWES 7.]

7. [*Geist*, "mind," also can be translated "spirit." In German this term is religiously neutral. It does not necessarily connote what Americans call "spirituality." Here its sense is more like "mentality."]

8. [The terminology of phenomenology is used. This philosophical method is based on the maxim that "things are given to consciousness as what they are." Phenomenology carefully examines the modes and contents of the "givenness" of objects in consciousness. Self-consciousness involves a distinctive kind of givenness: a feeling of one's condition from within. As Stein describes community here, she says that others are given together *als Gefährten*, "as accompanying." The individual *fühlt sich*, "feels himself or herself inwardly" as a member of the community. Givenness and feeling always carry this special sense in Stein's philosophical works.]

sion. Thus we have here an "organization" distinct from the individuals themselves, and with this we seem to be getting closer to what state is.[9] However before going into the question of whether the state confronts us with a special case of community organization, and what distinguishes the state from other modes of community organization, we want to bring in the third main type of sociality for comparison: *association*.[10]

The peculiarity of association, in contrast to community, is seen in the fact that in an association each of the individuals is just an object for the others: they are precisely *objects* and not subjects living together as in community. However this is to be taken *cum grano salis*,[11] inasmuch as we're dealing not with mere objects but with objectivated subjects. This objectivation presupposes a rudimentary perception of subjects, like that which is characteristic of the communal orientation. Thus the association can be conceptualized as a rational reconstrual of community. In associational life, it takes a distinct conscious act of will to call into existence something that turns up "all by itself" in naive common life. Community grows; association is established. Modes of community develop; modes of association are created.

Now the issue is, to which mode of sociality do we assign the organization of the state? It seems to me that this need not be an either-or question. Obviously if you're a proponent of *contract theory*, the dominant European political theory, and you regard the state as being grounded in a pact among the individuals

---

9. [*Staatlichkeit*, "what state is," is literally "state-like-ness." It connotes an intrinsic essential quality not captured quite so well by "statehood" or "stateliness."]

10. [*Gesellschaft*, "association," could also be translated "society"; however the terms "society" and "social" must be reserved for their cognates *Sozietät* and *sozial*, respectively, as in the very first sentence of this treatise, above. Stein discussed the contrast between community and association in an earlier treatise; see CWES 7:130-32.]

11. [*Cum grano salis* is Latin for "with a grain of salt" and indicates that the generalization does not apply absolutely.]

belonging to it, our question is already decided in favor of association. You take it for granted that there was a purely rational emergence, a creation by virtue of an act of will.[12] But this theory neglects obvious phenomena of state formation, and of the life of a state, that don't fit in with its scheme. If a conquering tribe merges with a subjugated people (as in all the Germanic-Romanesque states), then you cannot and need not talk about any contract among heterogenous elements that integrate themselves into the new entity of the state. By virtue of their superiority, which can be thought of as a purely communal relationship, the victors take over the leading roles and all the rights and functions they please, without any formal act of submission on the part of the vanquished and without a formal seizure of the sort that would be required for establishing an association.[13] They leave the rest to the subjugated, again quite naively, without bringing the demarcation to rational clarity or establishing it as law through acts of will. In the same "naive" manner, prevailing forms of law and civil institutions can be taken over from the ways of the indigenous population and become components of the developing pattern of the state.

On the other hand, there remains the possibility of an intervention of rational considerations and deliberate agreements as well as unilateral arrangements. Yet it seems that such deliberate acts have significance for the establishment and further development of states only if they sustain prevailing communal relationships, sanctioning them, as it were.[14] Obviously that needs

---

12. At this point we're considering contract theory only as a hypothesis of origin. Later we'll discuss what other senses it can have and to what extent it can be defended.

13. [Contract theory is challenged not because of any logical inconsistency, but because it does not fit the empirical evidence of European history.]

14. Schleiermacher designates the transition from non-state to state as the explicitation of customs into laws, and thus as a transition from unconsciousness into consciousness of community. See Friedrich Schleiermacher, *Staatslehre*, edited by Christian August

further consideration. But right now we stress this point: States can have just as viable a basis in community as in association.[15] Further investigation should indicate that the associational kind of organization never comes about until the state reaches a rather high level of development. (This is the opposite of what is taught by contract theory, understood as a hypothesis of origin.)

There's one more possibility to weigh: why couldn't individuals live in the state without making connections with each other? This possibility doesn't come up until we let go of the conception that sees in the state a mode of common life, and arrive at a view of it as sort of an accessory.[16] Therefore we'll postpone discussion of this until it proves necessary for us to break with this [conception].

Meanwhile we're sticking with the possibility illustrated by a glance at the facts[17]: states can arise on the basis of communal living. And we are inquiring into the distinctiveness of the state community—which means the community of individuals living in the state—as opposed to other communities.

---

von Brandis, *Friedrich Schleiermacher's sämmtliche Werke,* vol. 8 of the third division "On Philosophy" (Berlin: G. Reimer: 1845), p. 9. In the course of our investigation it will be established that this pertains only to the concrete basis of the origin of the state and not to its ontic fabric. See below, §3.b. [For a modern critical edition, see Walter Jaeschke, ed., *Vorlesungen über die Lehre vom Staat,* Schleiermacher kritische Gesamtausgabe, vol. 8 (New York: Walter de Gruyter, 1998).]

15. [Literally: "States can rest just as well upon community-like as upon association-like foundations." The adjectives *gemeinschaftlich* and *gesellschaftlich* are awkward to translate.]

16. [*Etwas Darüberhinausliegendes,* "sort of an accessory," is literally "something extra lying over there."]

17. [Literally, "by the empirical intuition" *(durch die empirische Anschauung).* For the phenomenologists, intuition was an act of consciousness that could be empirically observed in a further act of reflection. But that technical meaning need not be invoked here.]

*b) The relationship to superordinate, coordinate, and
subordinate social patterns; sovereignty*

Communities differ first by the number of individuals whom
they include, then by the manner in which they are anchored into
the individuals founding them, and finally by the relationships in
which they stand to other communities—communities that are
equal, subsidiary, or subordinate to them.

Let's begin with the last point. Some communities are
extremely basic communities, in the sense that they encompass no
others and are made up of no others. These [communities] are
families, in the strictest sense of the word, and relationships of
friendship. They can be engulfed and perhaps even intersected by
larger communities (clan, people, religious community, and the
like). So it's possible for the particular formation of the closer
community in each case to be extensively influenced by the fabric
of the one that subsumes it. Yet regardless of this influence, its
character as family or as bond of friendship remains untouched.
As far as this character is concerned, in principle it makes no
difference whether or not any integration into a subsuming
community takes place.

At the opposite extreme from these very close communities
is to be seen the one all-encompassing community of all individuals with minds.[18] Into it all other communities are integrated,
while it has no more [inclusive community] beyond itself. The
sort of formation it will have depends on the kind and number of
the communities integrated into it and upon their manifold
reciprocal connections. As for consciousness of belonging to this
all-encompassing community, it may be more or less developed,
according to the mentality of the closer communities and the
qualities of the individuals who belong to them; and the attitude

---

18. [*Geistigen Individuen*, "individuals with minds," is literally
"spiritual individuals." Stein's wording is neutral and inclusive.
There is no implication that the individuals must be religiously
sensitive, or that they must be mentally functioning at some measur-
able level of intellectual achievement.]

toward this community may vary. But these fluctuations notwithstanding, that supreme community *subsists* no matter which others
are integrated into it: it subsists *within* every closer community as
its basis and it subsists above and beyond all the closer ones as
their potential enlargement, which can be actualized at any time.[19]

Somewhere along the line between these two extremes lies
the state community. Other communities are included in it, and in
turn, it is included in others. But while the communities mentioned so far would be unaffected, in their specific character, by
the influence of their subordinate or superordinate communities,
with the state there's a limit to determinability by other communities.[20] This limit may not be overstepped without destroying the
character of state.[21] Aristotle will speak of state wherever "a number of persons has joined together into a community of life so as
to form a self-sufficient whole. . . ."[22]

---

19. [This principle affirms the fundamental solidarity of all
human beings. Anyone whose life is *geistig*—"rational," "mind-
endowed," "spiritual"—is potentially able to participate in the life of
any human community. This principle can override the provisional
exclusivity of a state, a nation, or a race.]

20. [In other words: families and friendships are highly variable,
depending on both the characteristics of their members and the
surrounding circumstances. Yet they are still essentially families or
friendships. But a state can be a state only within a relatively narrow
range of variation in the kind of members it includes and in the kinds
of larger entities that may include it, as Stein argues below.]

21. [*Staatlichkeit*, "state," is literally "state-like-ness." See note
9 above.]

22. *Nichomachean Ethics* Book 5, 1134a. [Harris Rackham's
standard translation of this sentence in Aristotle reads: "Political
justice means justice as between free and (actually or proportion-
ately) equal persons, living a common life for the purpose of
satisfying their needs." If Stein was looking at the Greek text, she
would have seen a form of the word "autarchy" there, but not the
word "person." The latter must be supplied in Germanic languages
to accomplish what Greek can do with participles.]

What interests us about this citation, in our context, is the stipulation of self-sufficiency ("autarchy"). It points in the same direction in which we were seeking what is specific to the state community. This can't be defined purely from within by the relationship, to one another and to the encompassing whole, of the individuals who belong to the state. Rather, what is peculiar to the state is that it must be outwardly delimited and secured in order to be defined in itself. What Aristotle meant by autarchy can best be interpreted with the modern concept of *sovereignty*—even though the two terms are not to be equated, as will become clear.[23]

The state *has got to be its own master*. The modalities of civic life may not be prescribed for it through any power standing outside of that state—be it a private person or be it a community superior, collateral, or subordinate to that state. Suppose there are two states, meaning two community formations originally organized alongside one another. Let's say one of them gets into a situation of interfering with the organization of the other and prescribing laws for it (be it by virtue of economic or military superiority or whatever). The sovereignty of the second is nullified, and so is its existence as a state. It is attached to the other as an annex, perhaps fusing with it into a whole new state.

Now let's assume that the all-inclusive community of minds would be organized in such a way that it no longer granted to the communities integrated into it any legitimacy on their own authority. That would cancel out the possibility of any state formation, as well as nullify all particular states in favor of one universal state.

Finally, if we think to ourselves that the communities integrated into states—such as family groups, parties, professional societies—might have the possibility of breaking out of the state organization on their own so as to remodel themselves according to their own autonomy, then the state would be dissolved from within, replaced by *anarchy*.

Those last circumstances give us more information about sovereignty and its constitutive significance for the state than our

---

23. See below, Part I §3.g.

initial determinations did. It's an inalienable property of the state that its actions and its laws originate from itself and not from any community standing under, beside, or above it; and that in principle, all law prevailing in its territory can be traced back to it (the sense in which this holds true is to be explained presently), and all acts of the whole must have their ultimate source in the state itself. And furthermore, it pertains to the state that there is within it *a force representing the state as a whole,* which is the originator of its organization and all its transformations, and is concerned about the observation of civil usages by all individuals who stand in any kind of connection to this state. If it has been said that the essence of the state is *force*, we see now that this old and abused saying can make good sense. It's correct provided you understand force to be the ability to maintain the autonomy of the state. This postulated force should represent the state as a whole. It matters not, for the inviolability of the state as such, what modality this force assumes—whether a single person is its bearer, or the whole people, or a parliament, and whether the different functions belonging to it ("legislative," "executive") are united in one hand or are divided.[24]

If preference is given to a certain modality of state, that didn't come about on the basis of any clear knowledge of what the state is according to its ontic fabric, but rather from the standpoint of an ideal of the state. But for its part, any such ideal of the state is not arbitrarily made up; rather, sense and possibility are imparted to this ideal[25] only on the basis of what a state is in the first place.

Now we must investigate [a related issue]: In what sense

---

24. Here too we find ourselves again in agreement with Schleiermacher, who regards the opposition between authority and those who must obey it as *conditio sine qua non* [i.e., a necessary condition] for the state, and [who sees] differences in constitution oriented according to who is the authority and who must obey it (subject of spontaneity and subject of receptivity, respectively). See Schleiermacher, *Staatslehre*, p. 23. [See note 14, above.]

25. [Literally "sense and possibility of this very thing are to be anticipated" *(Sinn und Möglichkeit desselben sind . . . abzusehen).*]

must the state, and accordingly the civil authority representing it, be the ultimate originator of all its actions as well as of all rights operative within it? Being the originator of its own actions means that the state has authority to command within its territory while standing under no other command authority itself. To those persons belonging to its sovereign territory, the state is able to give directives to do this or that as private persons or even in the name of the state. "Is able to" means that the *law*[26] is vested in the state and, in this respect, command authority and legal initiative go along with it (in a way to be clarified later). The state can commit itself to do something on behalf of persons and federations who belong to its sovereign territory, or even on behalf of other states. Yet it does this by virtue of a free decision. Nobody has the right to demand it of the state, provided that the state does not grant it on its own, committing itself thereby.

Sovereignty is not breached when the state takes such commitments upon itself in their particulars. On the other hand, if the state were to recognize a command authority above itself, that would be the abandonment of sovereignty and so it would be self-destruction. In an analogous manner, there can actually be all kinds of laws inside of the state that did not originate with it. But they are in force only *provided that* they are tolerated by the state. In principle the state could put any of them out of force and take in hand all organization within its area. If the state doesn't do that, and if it allows laws other than the ones legislated by itself to be operative in its sector, so that the right to make laws is expressly conceded to component federations or even to individuals, then this is a *self-limitation*. As such, it is not an annulment of sovereignty. Similarly, it is self-limitation if the state recognizes so-called *international law,* that is, if it binds itself to certain usages in its behavior toward other states.[27] We don't have the annulment

---

26. [*Recht* is "the law" as such, not any particular law.]

27. [In the time since this was written, about 1921, historic events have brought about a shift in opinion on the issue of national sovereignty versus international law. Stein is not presenting her own new theory here, but merely summarizing the consensus of her day.]

of sovereignty unless the executive power, the organ of self-formation, is limited by something other than the will of the state. In the moment when a force establishes itself over all objectively subsisting states and, on its own, sets limits to their self-formation, they are stripped of their sovereignty. But at the same time they would be annulled as discrete states and incorporated into the shared organization of one universal state.

The establishment of a civil authority is an act through which this authority sets itself up on its own. A claim is grounded in this self-positioning: the claim that only the law established and sanctioned by the civil authority should be operative within the area covered by it. Whether this claim will be implemented, and a state will actually come into being, depends upon whether the state is recognized or [at least] not disputed by the individuals involved. It doesn't matter whether this recognition or toleration occurs right away or whether methods must be applied so that the individuals settle for it. In fact, every civil authority will always need some kind of expedients to put itself in the saddle and keep itself there. Once again, in principle it is not significant what kind of expedients they are.[28]

Suppose there are two commonwealths (such as an empire and a member state), and one of them manages a portion of its affairs on its own behalf but is bound to the initiative of the other in everything else. This raises the issue of which of the two is the sovereign state. It depends on whose will sustains the demarcation between them.[29] Suppose that a state on its own has invested another commonwealth with a portion of its rights and of its command authority in its sphere of influence—and indeed in such a mode that the state itself can on its own enlarge, reduce, or entirely nullify this mandate, while none of that can happen without its cooperation. In this case, it remains a sovereign state

---

28. [The kind of expedients could be very significant at other levels of analysis, of course. Stein is still speaking only of what belongs to the ideal essence of state.]

29. [Literally, "The decision is directed according to whose will the demarcation depends on."]

and doesn't become a part of the other commonwealth. The dominion of the latter does not extend to the territory of the former, and it must have a different territory if it is to be recognized as a state at all.

On the other hand suppose a state, in the modality of a portion of its functionings, conceded (tacitly or explicitly) that it has no ability to do them anymore, so that it's up to another to say what's left for it. Then that state has ceased to exist and has brought itself to an end in every modality. Its sovereign territory has passed into other hands. The fact that the civil commonwealth as formerly organized retains a portion of its function does not alter this at all.

Suppose two signatories arrange jointly for one sphere of sovereignty and entrust it with civil functions whose allocation can be changed only by common consent. It will be especially difficult to decide where sovereignty lies.[30] Neither one can regard itself as sovereign any more than it can ascribe sovereignty to the other. Let's talk about this in concrete terms; for example, the German Empire and its member states. No state is sovereign if none of them has the right of unilaterally changing jurisdiction. If the individual states were sovereign, and if they had relinquished certain functions to the empire only by virtue of their own rights, then the Empire would be regarded as their proxy and not as a state [in its own right].

Conversely, if the Empire had complete discretion over the apportionment of functions, it would be a state; the so-called member states would be commonwealths entrusted with civil functions. [But] if only the Empire and the member states [acting] jointly can alter the allocation of functions, then the bearer of sovereignty is the Empire [when] organized in a certain manner. There's an internal commitment here, just as with a state that

---

30. [Literally, "If the two signatories within one sphere of sovereignty entrusted with civil functions can change the allocation of those functions only in common, just as they have set them up in common, then the question of the bearer of sovereignty is especially difficult."]

declares its constitution to be irrevocable. Yet there's still a difference between the two cases, inasmuch as in the one case a subsisting state pledges itself, and in the other case a state emerges out of others and right in the emergence commits itself, which means that with this commitment it enters into existence. In the moment of its emergence, the empire subsumes the states abdicating in its favor. They abdicate only a portion of their functioning, and this abdication is the precondition that makes possible the setting up of the empire. Outwardly the sovereignty is completely clear and beyond doubt. But its bearer is so complex as to be *"incredibile quoddam et monstro simile,"* as Pufendorf called the old empire.[31] And this monstrosity invites a breach of the law through which a "normal-shaped" civil authority could constitute itself as sovereign: either the empire, now no longer committed to any particular fabric, or else the original states.

Suppose two different self-proclaimed[32] civil authorities stake a claim to the same sovereign territory, as would be the case, for example, if the empire and the member states both wanted to constitute themselves as sovereign states unto themselves. An impasse would develop, since the fulfillment of the one claim excludes the fulfillment of the other's. Whichever one of the two authorities accommodates the real relationships is the one that turns out to exist as a state.[33] For as long as the dispute lasts and neither is able to impose itself, the contested sphere of sovereignty cannot [yet] be called a state.

Therefore, the existence of the state is tied to [the logical requirement] that a civil authority constitutes itself on its own and

---

31. [Baron Samuel von Pufendorf (1632-1694) was an early modern political theorist. *Incredibile quoddam et monstro simile* is Latin for "something extraordinary, resembling a monster." The reference may be to the Holy Roman Empire.]

32. [*Sich selbst setzende,* "self-proclaimed," is literally "self-establishing."]

33. [Literally, "Whichever of the two the real relationships adapt themselves to, demonstrates thereby its state-like existence."]

that this authority is recognized; in other words, it possesses the means to enforce its recognition and to punish transgressions of its law. By sovereignty we mean the property of civil authority, that it possesses the right to give orders throughout its sphere of sovereignty; only the civil authority itself can curtail this right in favor of another power. Therefore we cannot agree with the theory which regards sovereignty as an attribute that civil authority might have, or might not.[34] It makes no sense to talk about non-sovereign states. That's more of a periphrastic expression for a commonwealth to which a state has assigned or left a portion of its function, a commonwealth that may once have been a state.[35]

So far, the investigations have not yet touched upon one decisive characteristic of sovereignty. We will deepen our results when we investigate the connections between state and law. For

---

34. Jellinek, for example, supports this theory in his *Allgemeine Staatslehre*, a work we otherwise agree with on certain points and will bring in from time to time. [See below, Part I §3. Stein probably refers to Georg Jellinek, *Allgemeine Staatslehre,* 3rd edition (Berlin: O. Häring, 1914), pp. 486-89. Jellinek held that sovereignty was a historical category, not an absolute one, and he cited examples of medieval states that were not sovereign. Stein on the contrary holds that without sovereignty there is no state. For Jellinek, the essential mark of a state was not sovereignty but the existence of a civil authority. Stein seems to be responding to Jellinek's arguments and historical examples in this section of her treatise.]

35. This contested question illustrates for us that different "ideas" are confused in the conventional use of the word "state." Sometimes it means what we're calling a "commonwealth": a pattern of community, relatively isolated, with a certain organization for the life of its members and especially for the collective actions of which it is capable. On the other hand, sometimes the word [state] is used in our sense, where sovereignty forms the center point for the ontic framework, the point from which that framework is to be comprehended in its necessity. Below (Part I §3.e.) we'll work out how these two ideas relate to each other and how the contamination discovered here can be made intelligible.

the time being let's continue with the characterization of the state community. First let's establish a series of consequences that follow from the equivalence of state[36] and sovereignty. By talking about a relationship of equivalence, we imply that sovereignty does not pertain essentially to any community other than the state community. Communities that are not states *could* very well have the freedom to shape themselves[37] (for example, as the church does), but if that freedom were withdrawn from them (maybe from the church by the state), this would not affect their specific character. We could also say: The linkages and relationships grounding themselves in the essence of these communities *allow* sanctioning by laws (i.e., by positive law) but they don't *require* it. And along with this indifference with regard to any kind of positive-law regulation at all, comes indifference with regard to the lawfulness of their origin, if such lawfulness is apparent: indifference about whether it is owing to the commonwealth itself whose life it regulates, or to a power standing outside.

c) State and ethnicity

Furthermore, the equivalence of state and sovereignty entails the *detachability of civil community and ethnic community,* which often are taken to be necessarily bound to each other, if not held to be completely identical.[38] They become separable first in the

---

36. [*Staatlichkeit,* "state," is literally "state-like-ness," the essence of being a state. See note 9 above.]

37. Namely, in the sense that *factually* they are unrestricted in their self-determination. This is possible only if they do not lie within the sovereign sphere of any state. But if in addition to that they have constituted themselves legally as a sovereign power, then they are states *as well*—regardless of whatever else they might be.

38. [In German, the concept of *Volk,* "people," includes the idea of descent from one ancestral stock as well as the sharing of culture, history, and language. Stein argues for a distinction between this reality and the civil state. The German concept of *Volk* is in many ways the opposite of what Americans mean by "nation," i.e., people

sense that the ethnic community can survive if sovereignty, and with it statehood, is destroyed. The people can remain unaffected, in the distinctiveness of its community life, if it is deprived by an outside force of the possibility of living according to its own laws. (As an example, take the destruction of the Polish state.[39] This did not cancel the survival of the Polish people; perhaps Poland even became a nation to a greater degree afterwards than it was before.)

This must be further illuminated through an investigation of the special features of the ethnic community as such. But first we turn to the other side of the open question: whether a state community can also survive the destruction of the ethnic community. This can have a twofold sense:

1. Must the state be built upon a unitary ethnic community, or is it conceivable for a state to include a plurality of ethnic units complete unto themselves and set off from one another?

2. Would a state be possible which had no ethnic community at all for its basis?

The first question is answered by the fact that the existential possibility[40] of the state is not bound to the ethnic unit. The

---

of many heritages and languages who join together intentionally to become one. Stein will argue that a state can include more than one racial or language group.]

39. [Poland did not exist as an independent state during the nineteenth century. Many Poles of Stein's generation had birth certificates stating that they were born, for example, in "Russian Poland." Stein's family roots lay in that part of Poland that had been assigned to German rule. She recorded her family's experiences in *Life in a Jewish Family* (CWES 1:35); and she expressed interest in Polish political ideas and biographies on several occasions in 1918 in letters to her friend Roman Ingarden. Poland became a state once more with the adoption of a constitution in the spring of 1921, while Stein was drafting the present treatise.]

40. [*Existenzmöglichkeit,* "existential possibility," refers to the possibility of actually existing, not the possibility of being thought of without logical contradiction. This latter, essential possibility was the

national state or ethnic state is one special variety of state, but not state as such. It is very well possible for a series of different ethnic communities to become united by one force representing a civic unit embracing them all, a force that manages their life along certain lines homogeneously or even heterogeneously, without interfering with their ethnic preferences.

It's harder to decide the second question: whether the state requires any ethnic community at all for its basis. We established earlier that the individuals belonging to the state form a community. This is what Aristotle was talking about when he said that the state is held together more by $\varphi\iota\lambda\acute{\iota}\alpha$ than by justice, and that righteousness alone—without $\varphi\iota\lambda\acute{\iota}\alpha$—couldn't do it.[41] The meaning of $\varphi\iota\lambda\acute{\iota}\alpha$ in the context from which this citation is taken is rather uncertain, no doubt about it. But one basic meaning that is generally intended is that of community consciousness.[42] Some

---

usual concern of the phenomenologists. By contrast, existential possibility would gain the attention of philosophers a couple of years later, after Martin Heidegger published *Being and Time* in the same journal where Stein's treatise appeared. She introduces the term here. See Martin Heidegger, *Being and Time,* trans. John MacQuarrie and Edward Robinson (New York: Harper & Row, 1962). Stein's critique of Heidegger's existentialism originally comprised an appendix to *Finite and Eternal Being*, vol. 9 of CWES, but because of the great length of that work it was deleted from the German editions of 1950, 1962, and 1986, as well as from the 2002 English edition. It was published as "Martin Heideggers Existentialphilosophie," *Welt und Person: Beitrag zum Christlichen Wahrheitsstreben,* ESW 6: 69-135 (Freiburg: Herder, 1962).]

41. Aristotle, *Nicomachean Ethics,* Book VIII, 1155a. [The term $\iota\lambda\acute{\iota}\alpha$, "philia," can mean friendship or brotherly-sisterly love. Stein wishes to add this meaning to the term that she is defining here, *Gemeinschaftbewußtsein,* "community consciousness." The terms "justice" and "righteousness" translate *Gerechtigkeit* and *Rechtlichkeit,* respectively—both from the root *Recht,* "law."]

42. [Stein was careful to write *Gemeinschaftbewußtsein,* not *Gemeinschaftsbewußtsein* (which would mean "consciousness of

kind of community or other is going to encompass all the individuals belonging to a state as a whole, even an ethnically disunified one. However, this is not to be regarded as something constituting the state as such; that is, it's not necessarily required by the state's ontic fabric. The latter demands only a range of persons as belonging to the substance of the state and a particular kind of relation of those persons to the state as a whole (which is about to be discussed). The ontic composition of the state leaves open the issue of how the persons might stand to one another. Not from the composition of the state, but rather from the composition of minded persons,[43] is it to be made intelligible that—as we already indicated—[1] a concrete civic pattern develops on the basis of a[n already] subsisting community; or to put it another way, a ribbon of community winds around the persons involved in that civic pattern; and furthermore [2] that these ties of community are required in order for the existence of a state to be secured.[44]

---

community"; see below, note 47). Thus she avoids both the subjective and the objective genitive senses. Therefore two possible meanings of this term are excluded here: (a) that the community itself is conscious and possesses consciousness, and (b) that community is the content or object of someone's consciousness. *Gemeinschaftbewußtsein* cannot mean either of those things. The term, in Stein's phenomenology, seems to load the experience of being community into the experience of active consciousness itself. This notion is now to be explicated.]

43. [Stein insists that *geistig* ("minded" or "intellectual" or "spiritual") persons are the essential basis from which to figure out what the state must be, and not the other way round. To emphasize the direction of the logical inference here, Stein's long sentence cannot be broken up; but the numerals are inserted for clarity. As above, essence is faced off against existence, invoking the contrast between phenomenological and existential methods in philosophy. The essence of person, says Stein, has logical priority over the existence of any state.]

44. [Stein inserts two footnotes here in the same place, as follows.] The last remarks have a preliminary character and won't

The civil community requires—that's the main point—no ethnic community in order to be. Not until after we've conducted a thorough investigation of what ethnic community is, will we be able to decide whether, [in a case] where a state whole does not take several ethnic communities for its basis, the affiliation of individuals has got to be a specifically *ethnic* community.

---

become completely clear until the discussion of "state and law" [§2 below]. Compare Franz von Baader, *Grundzüge der Sozietäts-philosophie* (Hellerau: 1917), p. 7:

> Proportionately . . . with the vanishing of love, that is, of the genuine common mind between the elements of a state . . . that state approaches decline. It doesn't matter whether the disrespect (*Übermut*) reaches its peak sooner in the upper classes and only later in the lower classes, or whether vileness in the upper classes evokes disrespect in the lower classes; that is, whether tyranny takes a monarchical, an aristocratic, or a democratic form.

[Franz von Baader (1765-1841) was an eclectic genius whose writings addressed topics across a broad spectrum of the sciences and the humanities. He attracted quite a following in his day, and after his death his papers were published in the 16-volume *Franz von Baaders sämmtliche Werke* (Leipzig: Verlag des literarischen Instituts, 1850-60; reprinted Aalen: Scientia Verlag, 1987). Lectures on the philosophy of society appear in vol. 14, pp. 55-160, but Stein cites a separate, later edition of this material. Von Baader wrote extensively about mysticism and is credited with having rediscovered and popularized the writings of the medieval mystic Meister Eckhart. His anthropology and his critiques of the philosophers Immanuel Kant and David Hume may have helped Stein to clarify her own positions in the philosophy of the human sciences. Although von Baader's theological views deviated from Catholic orthodoxy, he is probably the first serious interpreter of the thought of Thomas Aquinas whom Stein encountered in her intellectual development. Of particular interest to Stein may have been von Baader's treatise "Ueber zeitliches und ewiges Leben, " *Werke* vol. 4, pp. 285-295. For translations of representative excerpts of von Baader's work, see Ramón J. Betanzos, *Franz von Baader's Philosophy of Love,* ed. by Martin M. Herman (Vienna: Passagen, 1998).]

A people[45] differs from the closer communities that we considered earlier—family and friendship circle—in this: [1] that with those, the foundation of the community was formed by altogether particular individuals; [2] that those individuals entered into the life of the community with their entire personal substance; and [3] that they all came in contact personally with each other.

(Admittedly, these stipulations apply only if you take family and friendship in the strictest sense of the words, and don't take all individuals who are kin by blood to be a family or all individuals who have friendly relations with one person to be a friendship circle. By family is understood here only the ongoing community of life, grounded upon a marital community or on a blood kinship. By *one* friendship circle [is meant] the ongoing community of life of two or more persons who are connected purely through an attraction rooted mutually in personal distinctiveness. If family and friendly communities are grasped in this way, then it's no challenge to the declared stipulations if someone points out the undeniable fact that neither family members nor friends always fully "understand" one another. Such more or less extensive estrangement or alienation is in fact to be widely noted, but in every case it represents a breach of the community concerned and doesn't alter the fact that according to the *intention* of community, the person is supposed to be taken up into it with his or her complete substance.)

On all these points, the ethnic community is arranged otherwise. It comprises an open multiplicity of individuals, so that personal contact for all those who belong to it is impossible in practice. The ethnic community can pick up new individuals without regard to their personal distinctiveness (at least to a great extent; limits obtain unilaterally inasmuch as not every individual personality allows itself to assimilate to every ethnic

---

45. [*Volk*, "people," also could mean "ethnic group" or even "nation." However Stein reserves the German term *Nation* for a special meaning, below.]

community).[46] And the ethnic community never makes the demand that the whole personal life of individuals is to be assumed into itself. But even if greater leeway is allowed here for individual personal life, still the tethers that tie that life to the people are scarcely less secure than the more tightly stretched ones of the closer community.

In the broader community, first of all, everything that constitutes community as such must of course continue to hold:

- it needs *one* current of life to be present, of which all individuals belonging to the community partake;
- it needs—at least in a portion of its members—one *consciousness* of community[47] to be present, encompassing the entire open multiplicity of the individuals who belong according to intention;
- personal contact of all members, which is lacking, must be replaced by a continual mediation of solidarity among those elements separated in time and space;
- every member of the ethnic community must bear the imprint of his or her membership in it, if not as a consciousness of membership, then at least in the fact that the member represents the ethnic *type*;
- finally, like any community, the people needs to cultivate one such type, forming the personal fabric of its members along certain lines, and one uniform *ethnic character*.

Now a people, in contrast to other communities, has one more essential concrete way of being itself.[48] A community having the

---

46. [The ethnic community *(Volksgemeinschaft)* thus assimilates adults, even if somewhat selectively. Being born into the people or ethnic group is not the only way to enter it.]

47. [*Gemeinschaftsbewußtsein,* "consciousness of community," is correct here. This is consciousness whose object is community: consciousness intending the open multiplicity of the community's membership. Compare note 42 above.]

48. [Literally, "essential positive peculiarity."]

breadth and scope of a people still cannot claim to be *an ethnic community* unless and until there emerges from its mentality[49] a distinctive *culture* particularized by the community's special character. A culture is a cosmos, homogeneous unto itself and outwardly circumscribed, of mental goods (be they self-sufficient objects like the works of art and science, or be they routinized modes of life concretized by persons in the act of living their lives). Each culture points back to a mental center to which it owes its origin. And this center is a creative community whose special distinctive soul[50] shows up and is mirrored in all the community's productions.[51]

The community that stands behind a cultural cosmos can in principle be more extensive than an ethnic community. A "culture group" can encompass a variety of peoples—at any given time and over the course of time. Similarly, smaller communities—like a caste or an extended family—form their own cultural "microcosm." But only for an ethnic community is it *essential* to be culturally creative. The community of the culture group can

---

49. [*Geist,* "mentality," also means "mind" or "spirit."]

50. [*Spezifische seelische Eigenart,* "special distinctive soul," is literally "specific soul-ish idiosyncrasy." In English there is no adjective corresponding to the noun "soul." Stein has not yet, in this treatise from 1921, affirmed a religious notion of the soul. The term soul will become increasingly important in her discussions of the human psyche in the early 1930s; see *Potency and Act,* a forthcoming volume of CWES.]

51. In my view, the chief merit of Spengler's *Decline of the West* lies in the strong emphasis on this symbolic character of all cultural patterns and its reference to a "soul" underlying it. This is so, independent of the self-referential historical relativism proclaimed in the book. This can be acknowledged even though it's clear that the disclosure of this symbolic context is in no way such an absolutely new thing as Spengler himself thinks. [The first volume of this two-volume work had just appeared in 1920. See Oswald Spengler, *The Decline of the West,* translated by Charles Francis Atkinson (New York: A. A. Knopf, 1939).]

perhaps be depleted, in that the peoples belonging to it share their cultural goods (or, hand them down to others in the course of time) and collectively feed on them without being productive as a coherent unit. Likewise, the smaller community won't be touched in its substance if it merely partakes of the cultural goods of the encompassing community without enriching that community, or if it cooperates therein only as a component of the greater whole and not as a self-sufficient unit. Peoplehood dies only with its spiritual creativity.[52]

In this "cultural autonomy," as a specific characteristic of the ethnic community, we find a remarkable reflection of sovereignty as that which is specific to the state, and [so we find] something like a material basis for that formal [right of] self-regulation. This casts light upon the connection of people [i.e., ethnic group] and state: the people, as a "personality" with creative distinctiveness, begs for an organization that secures for it a life according to its own lawfulness.[53] The state, as a social pattern that organizes itself on its own authority, calls for a creative power that lends content and direction to its organizing potential and confers an inner authenticity [upon it].

The question that sent us off on the last reflection—whether the state needs to have an ethnic community for its foundation—is one that we're now ready to answer. The issue is resolved by the fact that, while it's entirely conceivable to have a state that lacks this basis, a state where the only bond among those who belong

---

52. [*Mit seiner geistigen Schöpferkraft*, "with its spiritual creativity," is literally "with its mental creator-power." Spiritual does not necessarily imply religious. In other words, a people lives for as long as its ideas and ideals still have the power to fuel new creative endeavors.]

53. [*Nach eigener Gesetzlichkeit*, "according to its own lawfulness," plays on the word *Eigengesetzlichkeit*, translated "self-regulation" at the end of the last sentence, which is a synonym for "autonomy." Stein proposes that a people's own unique cultural creativity is a kind of law unto itself, not to be interfered with by others.]

to it is "loyalty" (in Kjellén's sense[54]), i.e., the mutuality of laws and duties in regard to the state as a whole, a state modeled in that way would [have some deficiencies. It would] have no inner existential authenticity, so to speak. It would always have clinging to it the character of something hollow and ephemeral. It might perhaps hold together for a time by authoritarian control, but not by any inner gravity of its own.

Earlier we accepted the possibility of a unification of several peoples into one state whole. Nothing about that possibility is canceled by the fact that each of the different ethnic communities has its own unique personality.[55] None of the ethnic communities necessarily requires a mode of statehood appropriate to itself alone. All they [really] need is a civic organization that takes their intrinsic lawfulness into account. It's only when civil law and ethnic personality are directly opposed to each other that the survival of one of them, or even both of them, is imperiled. That is no less possible with unitary peoplehood than with several peoples, one of which is favored at the expense of the others.

To this explanation let's append a few remarks about the relationship of *people and nation,* especially since much of what we cited as characteristic of the people is, from another angle, ascribed to the nation. Thus Kjellén regards the nations as big "individuals" with characteristic idiosyncracy that is attested in the developed personal type of their members, in the national language, in the specific tinge of "public opinion," and the like. Conversely, the people appears to him to hold together by the bond of loyalty alone. It would be hard, though, to apply this sort of definition consistently. If the ethnic community amounted to nothing more than the solidarity of laws and duties, then the ethnic community would be the product of the state and would presuppose the state—which Kjellén himself does not intend.

---

54. See Rudolf Kjellén, *Der Staat als Lebensform,* trans. from Swedish by Margarethe Langfeldt (Leipzig: S. Hirzel, 1917), chapter 3.

55. [Literally, "canceled by the unique personality of any individual ethnic community."]

In terms of "great powers" or analogues of individual personalities, you could regard peoples as nations. The difference, I believe, is to be found in this: that the consciousness of community which already is proper to the people is raised to reflective clarity in the nation; and, parallel to that, in the nation there lives an image of its specific uniqueness and this uniqueness is "cultivated," while the people only just *has* this uniqueness deployed in all its life and accomplishments, without itself being clear about all that, and therefore also without stressing it or adverting to it in any way. Hence, genuine nationhood is possible only on the basis of peoplehood.[56]

Peoplehood tends to develop into nationhood[57] if the people achieves a certain maturity. This is analogous to an individual person who becomes acquainted with herself only in the course of her life, without being able to say that she possessed no personal uniqueness at all before that "self-recognition."[58]

What the state demands for its foundation is not nationhood but a community of people.[59] Development toward nationhood is

---

56. [*Volkstum*, "peoplehood," ordinarily includes the meaning "ethnicity," although that may not be intended here.]

57. [Literally, "nationhood tends to develop within a peoplehood."]

58. Our distinction seems to touch on many of the same points made by Max Scheler in the second part of his *Ethics*. Yet ours is oriented in an entirely different direction. Scheler describes the people as a community of life, and the nation as a "collective person." Elsewhere I've discussed how we have to impose a distinction in principle between these two types. [See CWES 7: 276-78. The German noun *Person*, though feminine in gender, applies to males and females equally. Thus the sentence could read "herself or himself" and so on, if not for the clumsiness in English. See Max Scheler, *Formalism in Ethics and Non-Formal Ethics of Values*, trans Manfred S. Frings and Roger L. Funk (Evanston: Northwestern University Press, 1973).]

59. [*Volksgemeinschaft*, "community of people," also means "ethnic community" and has been translated in that manner up until

of interest for the state only inasmuch as it is of interest for the resilience of peoplehood. Therefore it's a bad omen for the foundation of the political system if sentiment toward nationhood does not reach a certain level or break out on particular occasions—for example, when there's danger that something might hinder the open display of peoplehood.

An objection against Kjellén's treatment of the relationship between state and nation arises on yet another score. The nation—as he sees it—first acquires a mental content for its life through the coalescence of the state; while the state in turn calls for completion through the "natural essence of the nation." The words "nature" and "mind" should not be weighed against each other here, because Kjellén does not say how he wishes to have them understood. But if you take them seriously in the strict sense, then it's impossible to face off state and nation against one another like nature and mind (or even "reason"). All community is the mental kind—that goes for a people as well as a nation.[60] The people has its natural basis, to be sure, and because of that, so does the state. But the people does not, as community, comprise "nature" and also does not need the state to complete it with some living mental content.

How is the line to be drawn between nature and mind within a people and within a state? Should a special "reasonableness" be ascribed to the state in a particular sense? This is what we are about to discuss.[61]

---

now. The sense is somewhat more inclusive here. Stein has stipulated her concept of the ethnic community: it is not based on birth, and outsiders may join it. Thus it is ethnic only in the broadest and most welcoming sense.]

60. See the treatise on "Individual and Community" in volume 5 of this journal [CWES 7. The word *geistig* means "spiritual" as well as "mental."]

61. See below, page 35; see also Part I §2.e. and f., and §3.d.

d) The numerical extent of the civil community

We briefly touched on the problem of numerical extent above.[62] We viewed it, along with relationship to other social units, as a possible characteristic of the civil community. What is distinctive about people and state is that they both include an open multiplicity of individuals [whose exact number] is not visible at a glance. For the state as such, there is in principle no upper limit on the size to which it can grow, as is illustrated by the idea of one universal state and by the fact of the Roman Empire. Alterations in the modality of state organization need only keep pace with advancing growth. Lower limits as well are rather broadly set: think of the ancient city-states or the Italian ones. The number of citizens must be only great enough to enable the state to have that self-sufficiency and independence from others that secures sovereignty. You can't put an absolute number on this minimum—not even within approximate limits—because for any given state pattern, what pertains to its military security as well as what pertains to its economic freedom depends on the size of the states bordering it. If one state lags considerably behind the others in population, then it loses the capability to secure its sovereignty, and its existence is left up to the pleasure of the others. Thus a group of little states can maintain stability among themselves, but as soon as the modality of the "great power" takes over, the previously viable patterns must expire.

The minimum population required by a state depends, furthermore, on the nature of the land, the mineral resources, climatic conditions, and so forth. This is because the number needed in the labor force to cover the economic requirements of the state, and to make it independent, is going to vary with those natural circumstances. We will have to discuss these relationships when we consider the significance of the terrain for the composition of the state.

The significance of numerical relations alters if we shift our gaze from the state as such to the people or to the so-called

---

62. See above, page 21.

"national state" established upon ethnic unity. Its extent is considerably smaller. On one hand, the development of a cultural cosmos requires a broader basis than the populace of a city-state affords. Despite the considerable intellectual and cultural differences between Sparta and Athens, we still have Panhellenism and *one* hellenic culture. On the other hand, too severe an increase must lead to diffusion of ethnic unity. The second is easy to imagine[63] and can occur in various modes. If the number of people grows through natural increase, without expansion of the territory, then the economic relationships compel a rather large portion of the population toward emigration into another state or toward colonization. The termination or even just the slackening of community life among the core stock of the people in the motherland brought about by this, plus the adaptation to altered conditions of life, will then lead to a modification of the original [ethnic] type and finally to the development of a new type.

If the national state grows through conquest and inclusion of new segments of the populace, then either it loses the character of national state, or else, in cases where the new elements are assimilated, the assimilation can bring about so severe a modification of the original ethnic character that you can't call it a transformation any more, but rather a *new* formation. Ultimately, an extreme spatial expansion will engage the various segments of the populace in so many different kinds of living arrangements and set them at cross purposes, that in the end a differentiation will occur that breaches the unity. None of these things are *a priori* necessities; rather, they're possibilities having the value of rules of probability, as opposed to factually historical occurrences.[64]

---

63. [Literally, "easy to render plausible."]

64. [Stein indicates that she was speaking hypothetically in the last two paragraphs (a single paragraph in the German text), rather than either citing concrete historical examples or framing absolute principles of historical necessity. Such absolute principles would be designated *a priori* necessities, in the terminology of Stein's intended philosophical readers.]

It's harder to get some insight into the necessity of [having] a relatively broad basis for the development of culture, which is attested by ethnic unity.[65] In order to understand that necessity, we've got to focus in a little more closely than before on the mental unity that we're designating as the personality of the people, and on the unity of one culture that corresponds to it. If we talk about one mental cosmos, then we associate with that the thought of a totality that is in itself grounded by the idea of a world of values, complete unto itself. The perfection of personality (whether individual or superindividual), just like the perfection of the cultural patterns that precipitate from it, is measured by its connection to the world of values. To the various gradations of values, there correspond various points of receptivity and specific abilities of the person; and in turn, to those abilities [there correspond] the discrete cultural areas. The unity of the person is attested in the uniqueness of his or her attitude toward the whole of the world of values, and it comes out in the coherence of all of his or her works.

The totality that we're talking about consists, for a single person, in a susceptibility for all the gradations of values. But he

---

65. [*Durchschauen,* "get some insight into," underscores Stein's phenomenological method. She is pursuing relations of inner logical necessity; she is not trying to detect relations of real causality. This method leads her to consider the reality of *die Volkseinheit,* "ethnic unity" or "the ethnic unit." In a way that is difficult to understand, the fact of this unity—or, unit—is said to "attest" (*dokumentieren*) the necessity of having some minimum level of population before a culture can develop. To the phenomenologists, the term *Einheit,* "unit" or "unity," stood for any one intelligible entity, insofar as it could be mentally grasped as one identical entity amid the living flow of the many differing appearances of its aspects within the current of consciousness. The unity, as such, is owing to the activity of mind, which assembles the unity out of the varying appearances and retains it as they subside. The unity of something (or, of someone) is that which is known first of all about it (or, about him or her), for phenomenology. We recognize: "Here is something. Here is some-one."]

or she doesn't have to develop all of the corresponding dispositions and doesn't really have to be creative in all areas. [The choice of] areas in which to be creative is [something that's] characteristic of his or her personal distinctiveness, as is [the choice of] which values to emphasize in practice. Suppose that there's no access at all to some area—it's not just that the corresponding disposition is undeveloped because of limited powers or particular life circumstances, or is purely passive and not productive. Here you'd have an imperfection transcending the obtuseness proper to all the empirical persons. You'd have a gap in the totality. With a cultural cosmos, you can't talk about a totality unless all of the cultural areas are represented in it by some works or some other objective intellectual by-products. Moreover, the discrete areas within a culture can and will be distinguished by the greater or lesser significance and originality of the works representing them. This distinguishing is the expression of the particular distinctiveness of the cultures and of the "personalities" standing behind them.

Now, what are these personalities like? The limitations of a private person, which prevent him or her from being productive in all areas, make him or her incapable of producing a total culture. Likewise, groups of persons who are united by their dedication to a certain area of value (such as religious communities, or economic communities of labor) are not capable of creating a culture: they will merely work together productively on it. Finally, the necessary mental versatility is also lacking in groups that represent a selection according to personal distinctiveness: family and friendship circle.

The community that stands behind a culture as a comprehensively productive personality must be so extensive that in it, to a certain degree, all partialities balance out and work together. For all the requisite abilities to develop, it takes a certain differentiation of life conditions for the individuals, and accordingly for groups of individuals, who are supposed to work as components in the unity of the culturally creative personality. Too great a uniformity of natural conditions, for example—such as what you have with limitation to the narrow territory of a city-state—seems to stand in the way of this necessary differentiation. We should get further information about this from investigating the interrelation between land and people.

e) Individual and people—individual and state

Before that, we still have a set of open issues to discuss. In order to mark off the uniqueness of the state community as opposed to other communities, we still have to investigate what particular mode the relation of individual and community assumes in the state community. Let's note at once that not all individuals need be integrated into the whole in the same way. This is so not only in the sense that they undertake different functions in the organism of the state, but also because a certain elite are to be regarded as "carriers" of the life of the state in a specific sense. In them dwells a consciousness of affiliation, a devotion to the whole, and a responsibility which the great mass of citizens neither know nor need to know lest the substance of the state be jeopardized.

The supply of carriers needed by the state varies according to its particular formation, of course. But for the time being we leave this undiscussed, and insist only that some carriers must be available. Concerning them, we wish to examine initially how it must be with their relation to the state. The relationship between an individual and the community to which he or she belongs can assume various modalities. For our purpose here, let's briefly recall them, in a very general way. It is constitutive for community as such that at least a portion of its members consider the community not merely as an alien object that they come across occasionally in the course of their individual lives, but rather as a whole whose parts they are and whose life is their life. Particular communities (especially the closest, of which we already spoke so often) have the peculiarity of claiming the right to encompass the individual absolutely, with his or her entire personal substance, and to absorb the individual utterly. The state doesn't ask that. The state allows its carriers the broadest latitude for their personal lives, which have nothing to do with the state's agenda. The state desires only to occupy first place in the lives of its carriers. Even this is to be understood in a very particular sense. The state does not desire that those who serve it and represent its vital organs would consider it the absolutely highest good. The statesman can be just as convinced as the saint that the salvation of the soul stands higher than the welfare of the state.[66] The decisive thing is that in the last analysis he lives as a member of the state, that this is the steady landmark by which he reckons and calculates his behavior even in matters apart from concerns of state.

In a state, many more individuals could satisfy these requirements than those who are in the "civil service," in the usual sense of that term. The greater their number, the more stoutly and securely anchored is the state's existence. On the other hand, it's possible for state office to be held by individuals who are not carriers of the life of the state, in our sense. The more widespread that situation is, the worse off the state becomes. Where state offices and institutions are turned into spoils of private interests, the backbone of the state is broken,[67] even though outwardly it might still manage a sham existence (perhaps its interests happen to coincide with those of the individuals, who are taking care of their own business).

This illustrates the Platonic-Aristotelian doctrine of the *forms of the state* and their possible degenerations.[68] In absolute monarchy, the ruler is the carrier of the life of the state and so is necessarily the "number one servant of the state." He carries the

---

66. [*Seele*, "soul," is used here for the first time in its religious sense. However, this stereotypical expression is undercut by the next sentence.]

67. [Literally, the life-nerve of the state is severed. *Lebensnerv* also means "mainspring."]

68. [Stein develops her notion of "carriers" of the life of the state, by showing how it applies to the well-known classical theory. The three forms of the state recognized in ancient Greek thought were monarchy, aristocracy, and democracy. These were said to be prone to deteriorate into tyranny, oligarchy, and anarchy, respectively.]

full responsibility for the life of the state, and there cannot be anyone else who stands in the same relation to the whole. He can harness all others for the service of the state, without making any of them its carrier in the specific sense. The opposite of the monarch is the tyrant, who treats the state—or what's left of it—as spoils exploited for his own personal interests. Whereas the consciousness of community that holds the state together is concentrated in the monarch, with tyranny the bond of community between ruler and ruled is ripped to shreds. With tyranny, each regards the other as an object, which means there has been the closest imaginable approximation to a relationship of unadulterated association,[69] bringing with it the possibility of an arbitrary destruction of the whole at any time. Solidarity in opposition to the ruler can unite those whom he rules into a community, but that community is not a state for it does not take on the form of state.

Analogously, in aristocracy we have a select circle of carriers of the life of the state who stand in for the whole, while its opposite, oligarchy, manifests a degeneration into a community of "exploiters" and a community of "exploited," or even into two special-interest groups, each of which is held together by its opposition to the other. Finally, in democracy, by its very idea, all citizens are carriers of the life of the state (whereby the concept of citizen actually is first defined and determined). Here, the state is resting upon the broadest base. But on the other hand, you've got the caricature that goes with it—mob rule[70]—the most severe atomization of civil community imaginable.

If you start from the idea of state, none of the forms of state that were mentioned can claim to be "the best one." The unity and integrity of the state seem to be best secured in an absolute

---

69. [Association (*Gesellschaft*) was contrasted with community (*Gemeinschaft*) in the social-scientific literature of Stein's day, and in her own earlier writings. See CWES 7: 130-32.]

70. [Stein uses the technical term *Ochlokratie*, transliterated from the Greek. Ocholocracy means anarchy or mob rule.]

monarchy, but only for as long as everything really is united in one hand. If the state grows to a point where for practical reasons it becomes impossible to concentrate the range of affairs of state in one hand, then monarchy is destabilized and the subsistence of the state is to be secured only through transition to another form of state. Democracy, by its very idea, gives the state its most secure grounding. However, it places demands upon the totality of the citizens that—when measured against the average caliber of human beings—are set so high that they are always very unlikely to be fulfilled. The danger of deterioration is very great with this modality of state.

Now let's consider what relationship to the civil community is like for those who, although they belong to that community, are not carriers of the state. The state doesn't need them to be clear about the fact that they belong to the whole into which they are incorporated in some mode or other. They don't need to grasp it as their own reality or take a positive stance on the matter. It's enough for them to fulfill the functions that fall to them without even being aware that these are functions of the organism of the state. On the other hand, it threatens the continued subsistence of the state whenever any elements belonging to it take a negative stance toward the state or regard it as a hostile power. If this happens, there has been a rupture in the civil community.

All of the considerations so far have examined the relationship of individual and state without taking into account the relationship of state and people. We've yet to discuss whether and to what extent the linkage of individual and state is founded through the linkage of the individual to the ethnic community. In principle, commonality sustains the latter bond [of individual to ethnic community] just as little as it sustains the bond of the state to the people. The unity of one "Prussian people" could not support one pattern, not even one that was a state in so eminent a measure as the old Prussia.[71]

---

71. [Literally: "A pattern (*Gebilde*) that was a state in so eminent a measure as the old Prussia was unable to prop itself up on the unity of a "Prussian people."]

Nor was the feeling of responsibility for the state [that was felt by] its most prominent carrier, Frederick the Great, grounded in any national feeling. Coherences *can* obtain here nonetheless, and it seems to us to be something normal and wholesome when this is the case. [Conversely,] the state that draws individuals under its spell—maybe they dedicate themselves to it in free devotion, maybe they're forced into its service—without being an organization of a people's personality (or something more) always strikes us as remarkably sinister. [It's] sort of like a machine that requires human life for it to be put in motion and kept in motion, yet does not come alive itself and remains indifferent about the life that it requisitions.[72] The state has no soul and no soul-driven productivity.[73] That's why it seems amazing—and in a certain sense incongruous, even though it's necessary for its subsistence—when soul-felt devotion is accorded to the state.

With a people, everything's different. But even here, there's no demand for a complete absorption of the individual into the community. Yet the community represents a commonality of productive soul energy.[74] It possesses inherent creative energy, the

---

72. [Stein's description of the machine-like state is reminiscent of the 1936 film *Modern Times* with Charlie Chaplin, but was written some 15 years earlier.]

73. [*Seelische Produktivität,* "soul-driven productivity," is literally "soul-ish productivity." English lacks an adjective corresponding to the noun soul. In the following sentence, "soul-felt devotion" *(seelische Hingabe)* is another approximation of the adjectival sense. There is no religious connotation.]

74. [*Gemeinschaft produktiver Seelenkräfte,* "commonality of productive soul energy," is literally "community of productive soul-powers." Such power or energy, operating in the realm of soul, would be available in a kind of reservoir, the community. ("Community" and "commonality" translate the same word, *Gemeinschaft.*) The term "powers" seems to mean common energy rather than private, individual faculties or virtues. Again, the sense is not necessarily religious.]

energy that precipitates out into works of culture. Individuals not only carry that energy, they have their souls nourished by it[75] (whereas from the state they receive only external benefits, which for that very reason are easier to observe). And so it appears to us much more natural and understandable for somebody to love his people and [to love] the state only in a derivative way, as its external modality, than for the state to be loved directly for its own sake.

Those last remarks should not detract from this fact: A state can have high value from the standpoint of community, even if it does *not* have a people as a foundation to rest upon. Such a state can secure the free unfolding of the persons and communities who are living under its care. Even if developed without reference to a people, a state can be the ready-to-wear garment slipped on by an ethnic community in the making. Finally, it's possible that the civil community allows the individuals united within it to become knit together gradually into one people.

§ 2. State and law

So far, all [our] reflections let the state appear in an oddly ambiguous light: it doesn't *need* the ethnic community as a foundation of its existence, but it *can* rest upon such a community and appears peculiarly hollow and ghostly when that's not the case. These relations will clear up if we try to shed some light upon what seems to us to be the central point in the composition of the state: the property of sovereignty. We are setting up the issue more broadly as we engage the question of sovereignty in the context where it belongs: as the problem of the relation between *state and law*.

---

75. [*Werden von ihr seelisch genährt,* "have their souls nourished by it," is literally "are nourished soul-ish-ly by it." Souls are not represented here as discrete entities.]

a) Pure law and positive law[76]

An explanation of the *idea of law* is needed here, as a preliminary investigation. Law can be spoken of in two senses. There's right versus wrong, as such,[77] which subsists independently of any choice and independently of whether or not it's recognized by any "law in force"—*right relations, period.*[78] [The

---

76. [*Positives Recht,* "positive law," refers to statutes that have been made at some time and place. They have been "posited" or placed into effect in specific historical circumstances. In contrast, law itself is something more basic that is expressed in those individual statutes. This distinction, familiar to philosophers, is invoked here. "Pure law" *(reines Recht)* is the law or the right as such. In German, *Recht* means both "law" and "right.")

77. [*Rechtssachverhalte,* loosely "right versus wrong, as such" is a term composed by attaching the ambiguous word *Recht* (see note 76, above), in genitive case, to a phenomenological term commonly translated as "state of affairs" *(Sachverhalt).*]

78. The sphere of pure law was first exhibited by Adolf Reinach, "Die apriorischen Grundlagen des bürgerlichen Rechts," *Gesammelten Schriften,* edited by his students (Halle: Niemeyer, 1921). The comments to follow are for the most part merely implications of his comments. [This sphere would be somewhat akin to a Platonic realm of pure forms. In phenomenology, to exhibit a new sphere means to describe a set of phenomena that appear in a way previously unrecognized and unexamined. The phrase *des reinen Rechts,* "of pure law," is related to the phrase *"reine" Rechtsverhältnisse,* translated here as "right relations, period." One basic given reality is affirmed by the two phrases in apposition: *"reine" Rechtsverhältnisse* and *Rechtssachverhalte;* two examples follow. Stein had been Reinach's student in Göttingen, and she edited his works for publication after his death in the First World War. Stein's own class notes were among the sources from which she reconstructed his lectures for the volume that she cites here. Reinach's work later appeared in another edition, in which Stein's editorial comments are carefully separated from Reinach's text. See Adolf Reinach, *Sämtliche Werke,* edited by Karl Schuhmann and Barry Smith

very idea of right/law includes, for example:] that any claim which arises through a promise expires through performance; that it's wrong not to pay back a debt; and so forth. Besides that, there's the law in force, the so-called *positive* law. Pure law is the same in all times and with all peoples; for it is eternal and does not enter into existence here or there or now or then. Positive law is created or put into effect through deliberate acts, and therefore can be as diverse as you please. That's why positive law can deviate from pure law. So the question arises why the designation "law" is nevertheless applied to both [and] whether it's merely an equivocation. On this score, it must be said: the discrepancy possible between pure and positive law involves only the *content* of discrete legal relations.[79] But beyond that, there's something that can be designated as *the form of law,* as opposed to that content. This is the a priori fabric of the law as such. And it is common to both pure and positive law. All law claims to regulate the behavior of persons. If a law is "in effect," that means this claim is recognized. Being in effect is something totally separate from the substance of pure law.[80] Going into effect is a mark of a *temporal* being, which begins and ends and, because of this, is

---

(Munich: Philosophia Verlag, 1989). See pp. 141-278 for the treatise cited here. It first was   published in 1913 and later reprinted separately (Halle: Niemeyer, 1922; München: Kösel-Verlag, 1953). See Adolf Reinach, "The Apriori Foundations of Civil Law," trans. John Crosby, *Aletheia* 3 (1983) pp. 1-142.]

79. [*Rechtsverhalte,* "legal relations," is a made-up phenomenological term. It is akin to the term *Sachverhalt,* "state of affairs." Compare notes 77 and 78, above.]

80. To avoid misunderstanding, note that this validity has nothing to do with logical validity, the validity of propositions. [The warning was helpful in German, where one word, *Geltung,* is used both for logical validity and for the effectiveness of anything that can become operative, as when laws go into effect. Moreover, the German word for proposition or sentence (*Satz*) resembles the word for statute (*Gesetz*).]

operative only within a certain range.[81]

Pure law and operative law[82] with the same content are related as essence and fact. For the law to be "realized," which means for it to be able to become an operative law, that claim must first be *made*. This can occur on behalf of its content—with pure law, namely, or even for example with ethical norms that are clothed in the form of law. It can also occur without such a foundation—*stat pro ratione voluntas*.[83] In that case, it takes a person to "make the claim operative," as well as a range of persons to whom the claim is directed and through whose recognition [of the claim] the law in question becomes an operative law. To *make law* or promulgate legal regulations means to make the claim operative.

The first law that must be made and recognized so that further laws can attain validity is the *right to make law*.[84] Every person who makes law thereby accepts the claim of this primary law.[85] Indeed, [the prime law lays its claim] upon the whole range of persons to whom its legal regulations are addressed, the range defined by that primary determination. The person can do this on

---

81. [*An einen Geltungsbereich gebunden*, "operative only within a certain range," is literally "bound to a realm of validity."]

82. [*Geltendes Recht*, "operative law," is the same phrase translated above as "law in force."]

83. [*Stat pro ratione voluntas* is Latin for "if the will stands in for reason."]

84. [In German, the word *Recht* means both "right" and "law." This phrase is literally "the law to set up law" or even "the right to impose right." Stein uses the ambiguity to craft a pithy maxim. It refers to the state's assertion of its autonomy in a kind of bootstrapping first claim. See p.62 below.]

85. [Grammatically, it is impossible to tell which term in this sentence was intended to be the subject. The better translation is: "This first law lays a claim upon every person who makes a law." Yet pronouns in the next two clauses suggest that Stein means to place "person" in the active role.]

her own, or by accepting it as a right that is transferred to her.[86] In the former case, if the realm where her law is operative is her *sphere of sovereignty*, she herself is the sovereign civil authority, and the sphere of sovereignty *within* which she is the "reigning" civil authority is a *state*.

All these observations still leave open questions. What has to be scrutinized before anything else is this: in what sense, and with what right, do we claim that the person is the source of the operative law? Let's start by trying to describe the character of law-making[87] a little more precisely. Enactments of law refer back to a subject who has enacted them and they refer forward to something that *ought to* be. They have this character of "regulation" even if they are not clothed in the form of statements of obligation. For example, according to its form, the statement "treason is punished by death" is purely hypothetical. But according to its sense, and apart from what is asserted in it, it includes a norm for the behavior of the individuals who belong to its operative range and especially for the behavior of those charged with the responsibility of upholding the law. If you want to grant the statement a hypothetical content, that content can still at the same time be the content of an empirical observation: that what the law prescribes actually is practiced. The state of affairs that would be given expression in this way thus would include tacitly co-intended information about the operative range of the law (where and whether the law is kept[88]). This observation has as its presupposition the legal determination.

It would be entirely different if you attributed to the sentence

---

86. [*Person* in German is grammatically feminine, but the sense is gender inclusive. The reference here is to a monarch: a queen or a king.]

87. [*Rechtssetzung*, "law-making," may be modeled after *Durchsetzung*, which means "enforcement." However, the term could also connote an assertion of rights. See note 118 below.]

88. The "where" need not necessarily signify any *spatial* location.

the character of a statement of pure law: the death penalty *belongs* to treason. This too would be a hypothetical observation, but not of a fact; rather [it would be an observation] of a relationship of essence. From this observation you would derive a normative determination and a practice shaped accordingly—not the other way round.

As already mentioned, the determinations could be grounded in [this:] that according to their content they coincide with a legal relation given in insight.[89] But in positive law the regulations are actually far removed from any hypothetical basis. They don't owe their content to any insight but rather to sheer arbitrariness. Accordingly, the "recognition" of a legal regulation does not signify hypothetical agreement. So in this connection it makes no sense to raise a question about correctness or falseness. To recognize a legal regulation means to submit yourself to it, and so to the law-making will.

b) The essence of law-making acts

In order to understand the possibility of this detachment of positive law from pure law, and of regulation from its hypothetical basis, we must briefly give some thought to the essence of law-making or regulating acts. We'll be dealing with a special case of those acts that we designated as free or "voluntary" in an earlier treatise.[90] The free act is characterized as a spontaneous realization of the I—spontaneous in the sense that the act owes its existence to the I itself.[91] The free act does not bestir itself to arise

---

89. [See note 79, above. The legal relation (*Rechtsverhalt*) is essential and so would be grasped by intuition, in insight (*einsichtig*) for the phenomenologists.]

90. Volume V of this *Jahrbuch*, pages 46 ff. [CWES 7: 52-60.]

91. [*Das Ich*, "the I," is the phenomenological designation for the point where experience originates. The term is simply the first-person singular pronoun, used as a noun, and it does not carry the psychoanalytic overtones that "ego" has in English. The I enacts its acts; it is the source of them. The term translated "existence" is

within the I and yet somehow independent of the I, as happens with instances of acquiring information or attitudes.[92] In what is commonly called an act of willing, [we find] an attitude and a spontaneous realization—a willing attitude and a resolve —ordinarily bound up together. And thus what is most distinctive about free acts is that they peg themselves to experiences of another kind—ultimately to attitudes—in order either to sanction them and unleash their practical efficacy, or otherwise to inhibit them. In all this, the I appears as the hub toward which the waves of emotional life[93]—ultimately emanating mostly from some kind of contact with the environment—can come streaming in, the hub from which a reciprocating movement, thrusting outward, takes its departure.

The entire occurrence can be played out even when the

Dasein, literally "being there." This term would later become a central theme in the philosophy of Martin Heidegger.]

92. [*Kenntnisnahmen,* "acquiring information," and *Stellungnahmen,* "acquiring an attitude," were discussed in the earlier treatise, "Sentient Causality"; see CWES 7: 47-52. See also note 133, below. They are not to be called free acts, since we cannot help knowing something or feeling a certain way about it. Although the I is affected, it does not commit itself in its freedom unless and until we decide to admit and act upon the knowledge (instead of denying or doubting it) or to affirm the value grasped in the attitude (instead of adopting a different attitude or none at all). This subtle distinction was a major original contribution of Stein's earlier treatise. It supports the phenomenological technique of the *epoch* . The *epoch* is the deliberate, methodological suspension of belief in the existence of something in order to consider its essence. This would not be possible if there were no difference between being conscious of something and affirming it to be true or right.]

93. [*Wellen des seelischen Lebens,* "waves of emotional life," uses an adjectival form of "soul" for which there is no English equivalent. This metaphor depicts the soul as dynamically mediating contact with the environment *(Umwelt).* This seems to occur apart from mind or spirit, and there is no religious connotation here.]

movement does not advance to the center and the spontaneity of the I does not engage.[94] On the other hand, spontaneity makes sense only within such a movement of the heart.[95] An absolutely "arbitrary" resolve of will without any kind of foundation whatsoever is inconceivable.

Yet the foundation can be of various kinds. It is possible for a resolve of will to base itself upon clear knowledge of a value relation that is demanding realization. (Such knowledge itself would in turn be anchored in a feeling.) In this case, as the I wills, it emerges as the executor of an absolute norm, placing itself at the service of that norm on its own initiative. Another instance of this would be when an aspect of pure law is promulgated as a legal regulation by a legislator.[96] This differs from a simple resolve of will in the modality of the effect. Here the effect is of a social nature and furthermore (in contrast to other categories of social acts, like a request, a command, and the like) not directly aimed at a behavior of particular persons. Rather, it merely prescribes a rule for ways of behaving that are apt to happen within a sector of persons.[97]

---

94. [The notion of the I as a central core was a commonplace in phenomenology. Alexander Pfänder had written at length about the degrees of self-investment possible for the I and the various intensities with which it could be taken over by influences from the environment. See Pfänder's "Motives and Motivation," *Phenomenology of Willing and Motivation and Other Phaenomenologica*, trans. Herbert Spiegelberg (Evansville: Northwestern University Press, 1967), 12-40.]

95. [Literally, "soul-ish movement."]

96. [Literally, "It pertains to this as well, if a law-maker issues as a legal regulation that which is a pure law."]

97. [The sense here is that a regulation applies to *kinds of* behaviors and kinds of persons, rather than to particular behaviors by particular persons. *Möglich*, "apt to happen," is literally "possible." A legal regulation cannot make it absolutely impossible to engage in the forbidden behavior. When people "break the law," they violate

The voluntary ratification of what is [already] commanded by virtue of pure law contrasts with the self-establishing of something that is not valuable in itself but is merely felt to be significant to me, or tempting for me, or the like, and is coveted by me. I can also set myself the goal of [achieving] that toward which the coveting impels me. I can even take something that isn't necessarily a real value nor any special real law, and make it into the content of a legal regulation.[98] You can imagine how "a law," meaning an embodiment of legal regulations, would be created out of the idea of a purpose that was desired or even just proposed as desirable. A civil law [could be produced], for example, from the idea that a certain class of people ought to get along particularly well in the state that it is supposed to govern. The legal regulations then would regulate all the civil institutions and the behaviors of the citizens in such a way that this goal would be made possible. The possibility of a positive law like that, a law entirely unconcerned about any [real] relationships of pure law, is beyond dispute.[99] It's an entirely different question, and one

---

a legal regulation; but this violation does not harm or change the underlying pure law.]

98. [*Wertverhalt,* "real value," and *Rechtsverhalt,* "real law," are phenomenological terms difficult to render in English. *Verhalt* in phenomenology connotes the way something is or works, just as it is, in the network of its real relations with everything else. (See notes 77, 79, and 89, above.) What Stein and other phenomenologists call "pure law" is a system of real relations that hold regardless of whether anyone observes them or even understands them. Value, too, is something that holds true whether or not it is recognized and affirmed. Law and value, right and wrong, simply *are.* They are not qualified as "for you" or "for me" or "for them." This brand of realist phenomenology would be quite at odds with cultural relativism and personal relativism.]

99. [*Reinen Rechtsverhältnisse,* "real relationships of pure law," was translated on p.38 as "right relations, period." It refers to laws that hold true whether or not they are acknowledged in any given society. These are contrasted here to arbitrarily chosen social

which we're not ready to decide, whether there can be any
stability to such a law or to the state that is fashioned by it.[100] For
the time being we won't address that question.

c) The subject of law-making acts. The state as a legal subject

Let's turn to the subject. A subject comes under consideration
as executor of spontaneous acts, and therefore is required as the
originator of legal regulations. Spontaneous acts are *free mental
deeds,* and we call the subject of such deeds a *person.*[101] Just as
free acts have other experiences for [their] foundation, so also the
personality exhibits other constituents besides freedom. We need
not go into that here.

What needs to be asked is this: Must only individuals be
considered persons and possible executors of free acts, or does it
also make sense to speak of "collective persons" and to claim
them as a law-making power? We have designated the state as
sovereign, thereby expressing that the state itself is executor of its
law. Is this merely a metaphorical way of saying that an individual
person has appropriated the state's territory as a sphere of
sovereignty (so that absolute monarchy would be the only
possible modality of the state)? There would then be only one
ruler, with one sovereign territory subjugated to him. But the state
would not be subject and object of the law operative within it,
comprising civil authority and sovereign territory in itself.

The state as a unity is possible only if there's a sense to
claiming the state as *a whole* to be executor of its acts. That unity

---

policies, such as a policy giving preferences to a certain group of
persons. See note 98 above.]

100. [*Bestand,* "stability," is also the technical term for "substance."]

101. [The term *Person* is always used with technical precision
by Stein. It is not a synonym for "individual" or "human being." In
German it takes a feminine pronoun, "she," which is followed here
to avoid awkwardness. But the sense is inclusive: "he or she" is
correct. See note 6 above.]

would be something other than the absolute mode of statehood only if there's a communal realization of free acts, [that is,] if a federation of persons can be the subject of them.[102] Let's start by assuming for the sake of simplicity that the totality of persons affected by the law-making would at the same time be the subject of the law-making. That means that this totality would promulgate all the regulations that are in force for it. If a set of persons band together, then each of them fulfills, singly and on her own, the act that makes up her mind in favor of establishing [the band]. But from then on, and in one [act of] realization, each one *with the others in common and for all* declares the alliance as subsisting, and precisely by doing so constitutes the alliance for herself and inaugurates its existence. Each of its subsequent decisions has the same character: The alliance decides, inasmuch as its members decide with one another and for it, and each grants her *placet* on her own initiative.[103] This "on her own" distinguishes the free acts from other communal experiences, for which it is unnecessary.[104] Yet that does not alter the fact that the community itself is the subject of such acts.

Going a step further, we see that not every one of a community's realized acts needs to be sustained by all of the individuals belonging to the community. A smaller body could pass a resolution for the whole community to which it belongs. The former then executes the act *for* the community—this is precisely why the resolution is to be regarded as an act of the complete community—but only *with* those who are currently involved in it and thereby united into a narrower body—with the entitlement to

---

102. [The German original of this sentence and the preceding one is somewhat unclear. In phenomenology, the term "unity" indicates one objective thing, as it presents itself to consciousness through the assembling of many variant appearances into that of which they are the appearances. A unity is what undergoes phenomenological analysis of its essence.]

103. [*Placet* is Latin for "it pleases." The word expresses approval and is a formal way of saying "yes, I agree, this is okay."]

104. From attitudes, for example.

stand in for or to *represent* the whole.

Yet with this, we have not yet gone far enough to understand in what sense it is that the state is to be regarded as subject of acts executed by the civil authority. The community of individuals living in a state is still not a state. The fact that its citizens form a community may be the basis for the state's existence[105] or may be a consequence of living under its law, and [in those cases] the community belongs to the substance of the state—but the state itself *is* not the community. When you've got a state, you've got an entirely new sphere affecting the life of individuals belonging to it and their community. But it's a sphere into which this life does not penetrate all by itself. The state stands in need of a person or a body of persons in order to make itself heard. It needs a range of persons in order to be perceived and to enter into existence. The state can execute acts only in that persons who "stand in for" the state execute them *for it.* Yet such acts have a sense only as acts of the state and not as acts of persons or of bodies that are not characterized as "agents of the state."[106]

It pertains indispensably to the state to be structured as a civil authority and a sovereign territory. It is essential for everything that is an *agency* of the state, which means everything that conducts transactions "in the name" of the state, to have representative functioning, which means to stand for the state as a whole. By contrast, that which belongs to the sovereign territory is indeed a *part* of the state and is incorporated in its substance, yet not an agency in which the whole is present.

Therefore the state is neither an individual person nor a union of persons. Nor can it be brought to life by the fact that persons form a union. The establishment of a state is an act whose sense

---

105. [The term used here is *Existenz* rather than *Dasein,* as above and below.]

106. [*Organe des Staates,* "agents of the state," is literally "organs of the state." Below, Stein will argue that an agent or agency of the state represents the state as a whole, not just some part of it (as the term "organ" might imply in English).]

requires that it be an act of the state.[107] Admittedly, the establishment of a state can be carried out only in the mode where a person or a body consents to be an agent of the state. For it's still the case that acts can be executed only by persons or federations of persons.

It should be noted what an ambiguous character these "representatives" of the state have. On one side you've got persons who execute acts on their own initiative, and on the other side agents of the state who do transactions in its name. They could not get themselves the status of representative independently, but rather they receive it from the state as sort of a "commission." (This is only a figure of speech, inasmuch as the state can hardly stand up and confront them with an act of its own. It does not exist "before" them, but rather makes itself operative only in them and their acts.) But then they must *take up* the status of representative on their own initiative (that is, *not* in their capacity as agents of the state). The same holds for every act executed by agents of the state. They accomplish it in the name of the state, but that can happen only inasmuch as the individual persons as such give their *placet* to it.

An analogous relationship is shown by the coordination of civil authority and sovereign territory. The civil authority (except in absolutistically governed states) is the body that actively constitutes itself, that passes its decrees, not for itself but rather for the whole state. The civil authority claims that it represents the whole state and that its law is in effect for the whole state, which means for that sector of persons who form the sovereign territory of the state and who along with the state are represented by its agencies. Since we're characterizing the self-institution of the

---

107. [Literally, "Establishment of a state is an act that has sense only as an act of the state." According to a phenomenological analysis of essences, the real being or essence of a state includes the requirement that a state must be self-founding. If it were founded by some other agency, then it would not be a state at all but perhaps some sort of puppet regime.]

civil authority as bound up with a claim, this implies that it requires the recognition of those to whom the claim is directed in order to become "legally binding." The *placet* of those who are to be represented expresses itself in this recognition. This "okay" doesn't have to be repeated any more in the acts of the representative body.[108] Through that body the claim is satisfied that these acts be regarded as executed by the whole community and binding for it.

In what modality can the recognition be granted? First, it's possible for the recognition to *precede* the self-institution of the representative body (for example, if a club elects an executive board) and to *entrust* the latter with representation. The self-institution then is founded upon that commission (it doesn't become something superfluous because of that). The claim to be recognized as representative is satisfied from the start; or more precisely—because a claim expires when satisfied—the self-institution is legally binding from the start. Therefore, there's recognition *in advance* for all those acts of the whole that subsequently will be executed on the basis of the legally binding institution of the representative body as such. And so a new *placet* from those represented becomes unnecessary.

Furthermore, it's possible for the recognition to be *expressly* given *after* the self-institution. (Imagine how a military unit might swear obedience to leaders who spontaneously took over the squad on their own.) Even in this case, subsequent acts are recognized implicitly as acts of the whole.

Finally, the recognition can even occur *tacitly* in a case were those represented always go along with whatever was decided by

---

108. [Literally, "the *placet* . . . that no longer will be current in the acts of the representing body." The approving act of the citizens is not re-enacted in each new act of their representatives, but it does remain in effect once given. A typographical error occurs here and again several lines down: *vertretenen,* "represented," should be *vertrenenden,* "representing" or "representative."]

the representative body when they are called upon.[109] A unity is formed by an act of willing and the transaction that realizes what was willed. In that I involve myself in the implementation, I simultaneously give my sanction to the act of will from which the implementation proceeds—whether or not the act of willing is completely clear to me. The situation here is exactly the reverse of the other cases. What you recognize immediately and identify as valid in practice are the discrete decisions. And therefore you recognize the implicit right of the community to make decisions. But the first [scenario above] continues to obtain in this case—the case that is of most concern for life in a state as it's actually lived: that every free act of a community or a commonwealth requires the sanction of everyone involved in it, in whatever mode that sanction might be granted.

And *that is the true core of contract theory.* This theory is to be rejected inasmuch as it asserts that the state—understood genetically—owes its origin to an agreement. It is also to be rejected at the point where it teaches that, by recognizing the state, individuals divest themselves of a right to which they're entitled outside the state—"by nature"—and that the state owes its existence to this self-divestiture of individuals (understood now as a principle, not as a historical event). There's no such thing as a "natural right."[110] Pure law subsists independently of all

---

109. [Literally, "in that what was decided by the representative body is always also implemented by those represented when they are brought in on it."]

110. [*Es gibt kein "natürliches Recht"* can also mean "There is no such thing as 'natural law'." Stein's objection is that of an astute philosopher of science. To the phenomenologists, "nature" is not some independent source from which we acquire rights or laws. Rather, "nature" is constituted by the human understanding, as a unified realm of events linked together through chains of causality. These coherences, the so-called laws of nature, do not exist "in nature" itself but rather show themselves to human beings who investigate phenomena of certain kinds. The regularity of the natural

individuals and their organization. There is operative or positive law only on the basis of law-making. This operative law can make individuals and federations alike into possessors of "rights"[111] and the latter no more originally than the former. For its part, law-making—as we saw—can just as easily have as its originator individual persons as federations of persons.

But contract theory correctly recognized that law-making, as a free act, can be executed only by persons; and that even if a federation or some impersonal formation engaged in law-making, or if it was done in the name of some such thing, every person belonging to that social formation still must be involved in it in some mode or other. In order to be able to establish itself and make its law, the state must avail itself of free persons, nor can it strip the persons who belong to it of their freedom. The state can make use of all sorts of measures in order to put its regulations into effect, even the sort that usually are designated as coercion and "false imprisonment." But all these are merely means for moving individuals to give their *placet*. They "motivate" but they don't "necessitate."

d) Regulations

After those last remarks, it could appear as though the acting[112] of the state were completely absorbed in law-making. In no way should that be said. We opted to stick with those acts in order to bring out with clarity the important cardinal relationship of state and law. For a supplement—also relevant to this question—it's now necessary to examine the other possible acts that fall within the realm of the life of the state.

To do this, we'll pick up on Reinach's distinction between

---

world is owing to the mind. It is *geistig*, not physical, according to the phenomenologists. Yet it is not arbitrary; it is objective.]

111. Concerning the sense of "rights," see pages 73 ff., below.

112. [*Die Aktivität*, "the acting," is literally "the activity" or activeness.]

regulations and commands,[113] to which we already alluded earlier. Both are social acts, which means they address themselves to other persons. But regulations do it merely in order to stipulate what should count as a law for the range of persons whom they are addressing, without wanting thereby to mobilize any particular person into any current behavior. In contrast, a command in every instance is directed to an entirely particular person (or a group of persons) and has the sense of setting in motion an activity of that person. This is analogous to the way in which an act of willing aims to set in motion an activity of the willing person herself. What intrudes between the act of regulation, and the behavior of persons over whom the regulation in due course gains influence, is the sphere of operative law, law which is made by such acts. [But] with a command, the persons and their manners of behavior are in immediate contact.

Social acts in the category of the command (commands were only an example for us to start with), where one subject has immediate contact with others, don't take a back seat to regulations in the life of the state. Regulations themselves, according to their sense, have need of supplementation by this other kind of act. Precisely because, as to their contents, regulations have to do with possible manners of behaving of persons[114] and do not pick out any current behavior of particular persons, there have to be special acts by means of which the regulations are applied to the

---

113. "Apriori Foundations of Civil Law." [Stein cites p. 322 of the 1921 German edition; see note 78 above.]

114. This may be the case in a very indirect way. Suppose a statement of positive law determines: A claim for payment expires after so and so many years. It's not aiming at some sort of behavior by persons. It merely regulates something about this objectivity—the debt. At the specified point in time, the debt expires on the basis of the regulation, without any further behavior by persons. However, the cancellation of debt—like any legal process—has *consequences* for a possible behavior of persons, and therefore so does the regulation that has to do with it.

behavior of the persons for whom they are supposed to be operative.

First, every proclamation of a law implies a command: the law-giver commands the persons of its sovereign territory to conform their behavior according to the content of the statutory regulations. The command is a conditional one and it could be temporally limited. It doesn't say: you should be doing this and that right now, but rather: if any of you now or in the future (maybe within some determinate period of time) gets into such and such a situation, he's got to behave himself so and so. The conditionality and time-boundedness do not cancel the character of the command as such: there are still the immediate focus upon the persons and the aim toward an activated behavior.

That command is entailed in every statutory regulation. But besides that [basic command], we've got some other acts to look at here. These are acts that are not required in every case as a supplement for the regulation, yet their supplementary functioning is designated as possible by the character of regulations. Regulations are there in order to be followed. That's what regulation means.[115] It's possible that the persons to whom the regulations apply are ready to submit to them with no further ado, on the basis of "recognition" of the law-making authority, and [that they] even know in some cases that circumstances obtain which are covered by such a regulation. Then no mediation is needed between law and fulfillment. The law (which is to say, the law in union with the aforementioned command that attaches to it) immediately deploys its efficacy in practice.

But it could also be that a mediation becomes necessary. Every command, since it's supposed to realize its sense, must be "perceived." But the edict all by itself, with nothing further, does not guarantee that the command connected to it will be perceived by everyone to whom it is addressed who gets into the circumstances that require its performance. To begin with, a statutory regulation might not even "reach the ears" of everyone to whom is it addressed. Furthermore, it's possible for the regulation to be

---

115. [Literally, "That's how their sense is realized."]

perceived as to its wording but not understood as to its sense. Finally, the regulation could be understood but without the insight that a particular case is covered by it. None of those instances would fulfill the requirements that are prerequisite for the perception of a command (in the strict sense) much less for its implementation. For to perceive a command *sensu stricto*[116] doesn't mean just to notice that something should be done. Rather, perceiving a command includes the entire concrete understanding of what it takes to get it done.[117] Nothing but the performance of the command should be left up to the recipient of the command (unless a certain latitude is expressly left open to him for his own initiative, which then must be narrowly defined).

It's up to the one who gives a command to make sure that the command at least *can* be perceived in this manner. So the state, when issuing regulations and commanding that they be followed, must bring it about that the regulations [1] reach the ears of the citizens, [2] are understood by them, and [3] can be applied to cases in practice. The first [task] is to be attained through a certain mode of proclamation of the law, which the state can arrange through commands or regulations specifically aiming at that. The distinctiveness of the latter, in comparison to [other] regulations and the commands that render them obligatory, subsists in the fact that they are not addressed to all the citizens but only to a limited circle of persons who are entrusted at any given time with proclaiming the law. For such representatives to be appointed is part of the content of regulations and, accordingly, the commands that follow as a consequence of the enactment of regulations at all.

[The second task,] to make the content of the regulations understood, is to be attained through continual *interpretation*. This interpretation must be carried out by the state itself, through agencies set up or at least recognized by the state. If the state wanted to leave it up to private discretion, it would risk having some other will intrude between itself and its citizens, or even

---

116. [*Sensu stricto* is Latin for "in the strict sense."]

117. [Literally, "of that which is prescribed for" the command.]

having its own will unintentionally misrepresented, and not being able to reach the places where it should be able to deploy its own efficacy in practice. In the former case, sovereignty would be breached; in the latter, faulty operation of the machinery of state would be the result.

The institution of agencies charged with interpretation occurs in turn through commands or regulations of the state. By contrast, the activity of interpretation itself is carried out—at least in part—in acts of another sort. According to its main ingredient, this has to do with purely intellectual acts in which the sense content—according to its determinations—is fulfilled and made explicit. Besides that, admittedly, every such "state authorized" interpretation includes a determination of the content, [to the effect that] the regulation to be interpreted *should* be understood in just the way that it *does* interpret it.[118] This factor directly rules out letting interpretation of its regulations slip from the hands of the state.

The [third and] last task that devolves upon the state in the interests of enforcing its regulations is the assessment of discrete cases where they have to be applied by agencies set up or recognized by the state, and the practical effecting of enforcement. Let's assume that the sole impediment lies in the faulty "power of judgment" of the persons concerned. Then the work of the state agency is a purely hypothetical task: deciding whether the case before it falls under any regulation and, [if so,] under which one. The transmittal of this hypothetical ruling to the persons who are responsible for enforcement would automatically set the action in motion. This situation arises mostly when citizens initiate a request for a decision from the civil agency in order to ascertain what they have to do. On the other hand there's the possibility that civil agencies use their own initiative to set about the examination of cases, and that alongside the hypothetical ruling, you'll need acts calling upon the persons involved to

---

118. [The meaning of this sentence ambiguous because one word (*Bestimmung*) means both "regulation" and "determination."]

comply with the decision. You'll need penalties and sanctions in order to bring about enforcement.

The interpretation of regulations and the hypothetical decision about the particular cases that fall within the realm of their applicability can be lumped together under the heading *"adjudication"* and contrasted with *legislation*—the original enactment of regulations.[119] As acts they are specifically distinct. The *hypothetical* acts that make up the bulk of adjudication are spontaneous but not in the same sense as regulations. What should be made into law is up to the discretion of the law-making subject; what we come upon as law is the law whether we like it or not.[120] Of course it's a matter of our spontaneity whether we will to execute the steps of thinking that are required for the interpretation and analysis of legal regulations and legal cases. But if we've determined to do such a hypothetical task, then we stand under the normativity of reason, which prescribes an entirely determinate path for the resolution of the task.[121]

What pertains to adjudication varies from legislative acts in another respect besides the hypothetical result.[122] Within adjudication, any hypothetical result is not really an end in itself; rather, it functions to make possible in practice the enforcement of legal regulations. The adjudication not only decides but also *pronounces a decision.* Thus it applies itself immediately to that

---

119. [*Rechtsprechung,* "adjudication," is literally "law-pronouncing." Depending on context, it can mean "judicatory," judicial," or "jurisdiction." *Rechtsetzung,* "legislation," is literally "law-positing."]

120. [Literally, "what we find as law is independent of our caprice."]

121. [*Normgebung,* "normativity," is a made-up word that means something like "norm-giving." Compare *Formgebung,* "shaping."]

122. [Literally, "What belongs to adjudication, other than the hypothetical output, departs in another direction from the law-making acts."]

which it affects, and it secures the contact that is lacking for regulations as such.

Immediate contact with the persons involved is something that adjudication shares with the other acts that we no longer attribute to adjudication itself, but which may be necessary to supplement it in order to achieve the enforcement of regulations: civil summons, warnings, specifically addressed commands, criminal penalties, execution of sentences. Insofar as such acts serve the enforcement of regulations, we can reckon them too as *upholding the law* (in the widest sense, encompassing law-making, adjudication, and "executive" acts).[123]

This brings up the larger issue of whether the state's whole life[124] then reduces to the enactment of civil regulations and their enforcement, or whether [additional] acts of the state are possible entirely apart from those.

The state behaves like an entrepreneur[125] [both abroad and on the home front]: outwardly in war, with colonization, with the forging of trade relations, and so forth; and inwardly with the foundation of schools and social institutions, the introduction of financial measures, and the like. In all such cases, it would seem, the state is functioning freely and independently of its function of law-giver. Here, more properly than anywhere else, it seems to confront us as *governing*. In this, it doesn't just prescribe mere modalities for possible actions, but rather it *achieves* something, it accomplishes concrete outcomes and places the persons of its

---

123. [*Rechtspflege*, "upholding the law," is literally "care of the law." It can also be translated "jurisprudence" or "administration of justice."]

124. [*Alles staatliche Leben*, "the state's whole life," is literally "all civil life." The phrase leaves it ambiguous whether the life meant here is that of the state itself or that of persons living in the state.]

125. [*Unternehmer*, "entrepreneur," also means "businessperson." and "go-getter." But see below, p.98, where "the state itself is not an entrepreneur."]

sovereign territory at their service. This is the proper domain of *the functionality of its command.*

The state can implement its projects only if it has persons at its disposal who lend themselves to this. But it's *the state* from which the projects proceed. The state assigns the persons their roles in the implementation. "Proceed from"—as with any command—therefore does not mean that the command-giver must necessarily also have the *intellectual* initiative. If the state lays its hand upon a private undertaking, then it turns into a public undertaking not through any alteration of the plans but rather purely through the takeover of leadership. This is the decisive thing about a command: its sense is that the behavior of one subject should be set in motion by the spontaneity of another. The one commanding is designated as such by the fact that the spontaneity lies on his side.

There's another kind of basis that belongs to the command, just as to any spontaneous act—such as the act of willing, perhaps, in which the subject commits himself to a future behavior. The way the act *should* run will be suggested to it by deliberations, wishes, and the like. The matter of the act is just the way it *does* run.[126] That basis could be handed to the one commanding as a suggestion from someone else. It occurs to him to make it his own, and supported by this, he now issues the command. The command is designated as a completely new action in comparison with its basis, and the one commanding is the absolute point of departure for the command.[127] In comparison with other acts that also aim to set in motion the behavior of someone else—such as a request, an invitation, or the like—the

---

126. [Emphasis added. *Seine Sache ist nur das Dirigieren selbst,* "the matter of the act is just the way it *does* run," is literally, "its concern is only the directing itself." The previous sentence was literally, "Whither it should direct . . . ."]

127. [*Auslaufspunkt,* "point of departure," is literally "point of out-running." The act that is the command is an act that originates with the one commanding. It is not caused by whatever suggestions or thoughts may have preceded it.]

command is distinguished by the fact that there [with those other acts], the inciting subject and the implementing subject, with their spontaneity, are both involved; while here [with the command], spontaneity lies entirely on the side of the inciting subject. There [with requests or invitations] you've got two actions, of which one is motivated by the other. Here [with commands] you've got a single action. To put it succinctly—what the person who implements "does" is effectuated by the person commanding, through what the implementing person does.

Of course—as emphasized already above—the freedom of a person is never to be excluded. But in the case of a command, the situation is such that the consent of the one implementing is already presupposed; [he consents] to put himself at the disposal of the one commanding as an agent of his will. His freedom comes to expression in this consent. It no longer has any function in this connection: issue a command—receive it—carry it out. That is not to say that this consent must have temporally preceded, or maybe that an express act of submission to the will of the one commanding had to have taken place. This is merely a matter of a *practical* prerequisite that is to be deduced from the sense of the command. The *sense* of command *as command* is not purely satisfied if, between reception and implementation, there intervenes a deliberation whether you should or should not obey, and a free decision based upon that. (Naturally, this does not exclude that such behavior can on reasonable grounds be offered with respect to a command. Then the defect lies on the side of the command: either in its content or in the fact that the presuppositions appropriate for the issuance of the command are not even present.)

Where the preconditions for the issuance of commands prevail, a relationship of *control* subsists. Being under the command of another is incompatible with *sovereignty*. This is why we must say that it belongs irrevocably to a state to execute its acts *on its own initiative* and in doing so to be bound to no other will. But toward clarifying the concept of sovereignty, there's still more to be gathered from the sense of command. To say that the state controls itself is to say that it controls the persons in its territory.[128] It can allow them the freedom to be active on their own, and can allow relationships of control to subsist among them. But the state must retain for itself the possibility of pulling them into the service of its actions. There should be within its sphere, meaning between the persons who belong to the state and a command authority standing beyond the state, no relation of control that is inviolable with regard to the state.[129] Relationships of control subsist only to the extent that the state tolerates them, and they can at any time be suspended by it. In principle, the state is the central office in which is vested the leadership of the total activity within its territory. It's up to the state to decide how broadly it actually wants to make use of it.

Let's designate the commanding acts of the state as acts of *governing*. And we must say that they belong to the state just as essentially as does law-making. The two functions reciprocally require one another. Regulations are dependent upon acts of government for their enforcement. And those acts of government which do not stand at the service of regulations require on their side occasional legal regulations as an instrument of their enforcement: regulations concerning the institution of agencies for certain actions of government, for the distribution of its functions, and so forth.

This brings up a question to examine. Are we dealing with two manners of activation of the state that are parallel, in the strict sense, and independent in character, and integrated complementarily only in a concrete political system? Or does an even more basic fundamental connection subsist? It's important to figure this out, because the relationship between state and law is determined accordingly. We've already seen that a command is bound up with every act of regulation on the side of the state. And from that

---

128. [Literally, "That the state has itself in hand goes with the fact that it has the persons of its territory in hand."]

129. [Stein is describing what is logically entailed in the notion of a state. She does not mean to assert that such a state ought to exist. Her arguments here in no way call for the establishment of such an absolutist regime.]

alone, it's also clear that governing is the real life of the state. But could there be such a thing as a state that did nothing else but govern and while doing so never supported itself with any operative law? We haven't yet convinced ourselves of that.

When the state issues commands, it doesn't thereby mean to proceed arbitrarily. That is, the *content* of the commands is indeed placed at its discretion, but it claims as its *right* the issuing of commands as such.[130] To be a state means to have the right to do what you want with your sovereign territory,[131] that is, to command freely. Earlier we said "the first law that is made is the law to make laws."[132] Now we must add: " . . . and to govern." You might think you could argue like this: If the right to govern and to make laws is made, then even this act of making proceeds from the law, and the state is therefore activating itself in a manner still unlawful. However, that way of thinking is misleading. Don't imagine a *temporal* precedence for the "presupposed" law-making at all. Whenever the state carries out an act—whether it's law-making or a command—according to its own *sense* it must claim this as its right. State and [that] right come to life together. This means, where there's a state, there is according to the [very] idea also a positive law at hand, even if not a single legal regulation has yet been pronounced. Conversely, when you have a positive law, a state also is necessary as its ultimate source, even if a civil authority has yet to establish itself [and] claim for itself the ultimate decision in legal matters.

No other act belongs so irrevocably to the life of the state as do command and regulation. What we mentioned earlier: request-

---

130. [*Recht,* "right," is the same word as "law" at the end of the preceding paragraph. The choice of how to translate the word always depends on the context. See note 132, below.]

131. [Literally, "to have its sovereign territory at its disposal."]

132. [Stein slightly misquotes herself, playing with the ambiguity of the two meanings of *Recht.* She wrote on page 40 above: "The first law that must be made and recognized so that further laws can attain validity is the right to make law (*das Recht, Recht zu setzen*)."]

ing, warning, and the like, [are acts that] the state is free to do. Occasionally they serve to assist in the enforcement of commands and regulations. You resort to them in order to overcome possible "frictions," but in principle it's conceivable for the life of the state to proceed without friction so that such means of assistance would not be required. A qualification is still necessary here in favor of the acts that—like punishing—are to be regarded as practical legal measures. They are surely of secondary importance in comparison with regulations and commands, but they belong to the realm of acts that the state must in principle reserve to itself and that can be carried out by others only with its authorization, express or tacit.

Something analogous holds for all acts that set up a liaison with other states. In principle, they are a matter for the state and not for private persons. This ought not to be misunderstood: to be interested in other states, to research their idiosyncrasies and their history and the like, to admire or to loathe them—naturally that is left up to individuals. Conceivably some state could forbid this (to the extent that a prohibition makes sense, which is not the case with admiration, for example.) But such a prohibition cannot be justified by an appeal to what the state as such must claim for itself. What we had in mind, as the domain reserved to the state in principle, would be more like acts that have as their result a commitment binding upon the state, which means acts having legal effect (like settlement of a contract) and those that work toward that (negotiations and the like).

No explanation is needed to show that such acts can be executed only by the state, inasmuch as they are supposed to have as their consequence a commitment binding upon the state. On the other hand, where dealing with a commitment binding upon private persons, we've got to look into [the question of] whether the state is involved too. Without doubt, sovereignty would be breached if citizens of the state were to take upon themselves, without its concurrence, obligations that the state could not alter. Thus, where you have a state in the full sense of the word, the citizens [acting] apart from it cannot make a binding commitment to outsiders. This does not mean that ongoing cooperation is required in every single case. Substituting for this, the state can issue regulations that once and for all prescribe, and thereby also effectuate, which acts of its citizens have binding power and which do not. From then on, those acts for which the state—by means of its regulations—refuses its consent are null and void. And this affects not only those acts that, considered in themselves, would be legal but are declared invalid by the state, but also even those that serve as preliminaries for them.

All the acts that we recognized as belonging to the specific domain of the state were *social*. We must investigate whether there's any significance to this in principle. With what we designated as adjudication, we found an ingredient that is inseparable from the social or other-personal factor:[133] the interpretation of regulations and the evaluation of cases, insofar as a purely intellectual performance is to be seen in these. We've already seen that the specific domain of the state does not include intellectual activity or any information-uptake or stance-acquisition at all.[134] When you're talking about *spontaneous* acts—such as the articulated steps of thinking that are required for the preparation of certain information—it might still be meaningful to talk about an intervention by the state. Other than that, the acts not only are none of its business, but also are in principle beyond its reach, just as they are beyond the reach of any arbitrary intervention at all.

It's a further question whether the state has any access at all to this area, which is not its proper domain, and whether it is

---

133. [*Bestand*, "ingredient," also means "substance." *Fremdpersonal*, "other-personal," is a made-up word. In this context, it probably refers to the fact that many different persons exist besides myself. Another meaning is possible but less likely: that "the social" is something different from "the personal."]

134. [*Kenntnisnahmen*, "information-uptake," and *Stellungnahmen*, "attitude acquisition," are regarded by Stein as relatively passive experiences that seem just to happen to a person without any particular decision or effort. They contrast with "spontaneous acts" in the next sentence, which require the person's initiative. See note 92 above.]

capable on its own of having information and attitudes. We already know that all acts of the state have to be carried out by persons or groups of persons who represent it. But it could be that the "representation" does not have the same sense for all kinds of acts. Where we have representation *sensu stricto*[135] we could say: The state carries out the acts in question *through* its representative. *It* is their subject. Therefore the state can choose, command, regulate, promise, commit itself, and so on. Can you also say, in the same way, that the state thinks or deliberates, it gets angry, it feels sad, and the like? Obviously—in contrast to the cases mentioned above—it's a mere *façon de parler* if you use such an idiom.[136]

Information-uptake and attitude-acquisition are required as a basis for the acts that the state carries out. But to come into possession of these is the business of persons who belong to the realm of the state. It must avail itself of them for this purpose. Or it can recruit them specifically for it. Then it's they who perceive, judge, feel, and have an attitude on behalf of the state. But you can't say that the state itself is doing it through them. Therefore, the proper life of the state is limited to the *sphere of freedom,* period. (This even excludes those acts that, having a moment of spontaneity in themselves, stand in service of passive acts—as does information-uptake—and maybe acts of thought.)

You can't just say that any act claiming to be an act of the state has got to be an act of a *social* nature. For example, a decision need not be addressed to any person at all. However, it belongs to the essence of state acts that even the ones deprived of such an address have a certain social effect, [whether] immediate or mediated.

At some point we should follow up the implications of what we've established concerning the acts belonging in principle to the life of the state, and their [role as a] basis for the development of civil agencies. It's time now to delve into [another issue]: in what does the proper life of the state as such consist.

---

135. [*Sensu stricto* is Latin for "in the strict sense."]

136. [*Façon de parler* is French for "manner of speaking."]

e) Sovereignty as conditio sine qua non *of the state*[137]

Everything that we've established so far serves to illuminate sovereignty, and therefore the essence of the state, in a brighter light. Sovereignty, as the self-configuration of a commonwealth, and freedom of an individual person [are concepts that] belong together inseparably.[138] Only a formation that involves free persons can declare itself to be sovereign or can exhibit sovereignty in practice. The constitutive threshold for sovereignty is that the freedom of individuals is not destroyed by the will of this formation, or of the body representing it, but instead remains a condition of putting that will into effect. This threshold is not to be regarded as a limitation of sovereignty. "Unlimited civil authority" essentially subsists to the precise extent that it is recognized, and it can be wiped out at any moment. The warrant for its subsistence is provided by the motives that back up its recognition. And this comprises the peculiar contingency that the state has about it: what makes it into a state—its legal nature—is unable to guarantee its existence. The latter is secured by a foundation that is extrinsic to its essence.

You get the strongest security when the federation of persons that is caught up into the state already has been getting along as a community beforehand, and when the law that the state makes is merely a sanction of the community relationships emerging originally, or at least follows the tendencies of community life. Finally, [the state is secure] when the individual or the body that constitute themselves as the civil authority appear to be the qualified leaders [in the eyes of] the persons who belong to their sovereign territory, and preferably, to be sure, in [so] self-evident a manner that the legitimacy of the leadership does not become a problem.

---

137. [*Conditio sine qua non* is a technical term in philosophy. It means "necessary condition" or, literally, "condition without which not."]

138. [*Gemeinwesen,* "commonwealth," is literally "common essence." Compare *Gemeinschaft,* "community."]

If these foundations for a healthy political system are lacking, then there can, in principle, emerge in its place a *coercive instrumentality* which restores civil authority so as to secure recognition for itself in the sphere of control to which it lays claim, and to extort it from resisting individuals through some pressure. This is possible *in principle*—that means, such a state would not be any less a *state*. Such coercive instrumentalities will never *in fact* be capable of entirely displacing other safeguards, just as on the other hand we can scarcely do without them as a back-up.

Finally, our arguments result in an answer to the question of who the *carrier of sovereignty* might be. This has become controversial in quite a number of ways. On one side stand the theoreticians of absolute monarchy, who claim this for the monarch. On the other side, the proponents of popular sovereignty ascribe it to the totality of the individuals belonging to the state (whether as an inalienable property or as one that they can or even must relinquish in favor of a monarch or a representative body, it's all the same). Both parties are mistaken. The state, or the civil authority that embodies it, is sovereign, but those who currently hold that authority are not.[139] If the whole people constitutes itself as civil authority, then the sovereignty rests with the people. If it is a monarch [that does so], then sovereignty appears concentrated in his hands. Sovereignty always presupposes a claim of control and its satisfaction through the recognition of those involved. It does not accrue "originally" either to the one side or to the other. And if the ruler and the ruled coincide, that's a special case without significance in principle. Therefore what we already established earlier is confirmed: the idea of the state [as such] does not favor any one of the possible modalities of state over the others.

We have been trying to understand sovereignty by considering its connections with the freedom of the individuals who form the foundation of the state. These connections put us in mind of

---

139. [Literally, "but not the possessors of it."]

an analogy that suggests itself even before we've checked out the foundational relationships.

f) The state as a legal entity[140]

Sovereignty plays a role in the composition of the state that is analogous to that of freedom in the fabric of the individual person. We call the person free inasmuch as she is the executor of spontaneous acts and therein governs herself. And this freedom is inseparable from personhood.[141] Sovereignty is freedom in the same sense, the only difference being that what is governing itself here is a social whole, so all acts are modified accordingly. And if the state is deprived of its sovereignty and subjugated to the commands of another, then it is stripped of its statehood, in the same way that an individual is stripped of personhood when his spontaneity is suspended and he is shackled to the will of another.[142]

---

140. [*Juristische Person,* a technical term equivalent to "legal entity," is literally "juridical person" and is translated as such below. Stein is examining the extent of the analogy between the state and the human person as to their respective components and capabilities. In German the noun *Person* is grammatically feminine but its sense is gender inclusive. It would be correct, but awkward, in English to refer back to this noun with double pronouns: "he or she," "himself or herself." Yet to use only the masculine pronouns here would suggest to speakers of American English a gender exclusivity that is foreign to Stein's text. In fact, Stein plays off the masculine forms corresponding to "state" against the feminine forms corresponding to "person."]

141. [Literally, "the personality." Personhood (*Personalität*) is made parallel to statehood (*Staatlichkeit*). Both terms connote that which pertains to essence, and are used in a sense that differs somewhat from the ordinary usage of their English equivalents.]

142. [As a phenomenologist, Stein is speaking here of essences, not of real human individuals. In other words: when the idea of freedom is subtracted from the idea of an individual, the remainder

The parallel between personal freedom and state sovereignty lets us understand why we're prone to claim that the state is a "person," but not so much the people, even though the people seems to approximate individual personhood more closely in other respects (think of distinctive character traits). The people —according to its essential substance—is a community of persons and it can perform free acts. But freedom, which is the specific mark of personhood, does not play the same constitutive role in the case of the people as it does in the case of the state. The life of the people transpires for the most part in the modality of opinion and impulse.[143] The life of the state transpires entirely within the realm of freedom and is completely taken up in free acts. Wherever we come upon the state it confronts us in free acts, and [it confronts us] precisely as a unity assembled out of those acts.[144] This very much resembles the individual person, where the distinctiveness of the personal unity is plainly documented in the volition, the behavior, and all the other manners of comportment by which the person keeps herself firmly in hand when, for example, she is absorbed in conditions, inclinations, attitudes and such that can be and usually are diverse and conflicting.

With all of this, we see in turn that it's impossible to think of the state as complete unto itself;[145] [we see] its reliance upon a foundation of another kind. An individual person cannot will or

---

is less than the idea of person. Stein's argument here does not say that coercion applied to a real, existing human person would wipe out the personhood of that person.]

143. [*Stellungnahmen und triebhaftem Tun,* "opinion and impulse," is literally "attitude-uptake and impulsive doing."]

144. [In phenomenology, a unity is what can be known. It is the object that appears to consciousness through a coalescence of multiple impressions from various perspectives at different times into one "this."]

145. [Literally, "the impossibility of completing the state in itself." Stein is examining the essence or sense of a state as such; she is not describing actual states.]

behave in isolation—because some impetus is needed—nor are the actions of the state conceivable without the diverse agitation of a living community to give them content and direction.

[On one hand,] by their distinctive fabric, free acts are bound up inextricably with individuality. On the other hand, the distinctiveness of life in a state is that it goes on in the modality of free acts. [Taken together] this lets us understand that the state demands a unified leadership.[146] Every free act—and surely the deliberate decision as well as the doing that brings it to execution—requires a push, a *"fiat!"*.[147] And this is always the business of an individual person. So every state action must also be initiated by an individual person. Jellinek distinguishes between monarchy and republic according to whether the will of the state appears as that of an "individual, particular, visible, living person" or "merely as a will of a committee possessing only juridical reality."[148] For the time being let's not ask what "juridical reality" means. Let's just establish that in the republic as well as in the monarchy, every action of the state has to have an individual person who sets it in motion. It doesn't always have to be—as in monarchy—the same person in whom "all functions of the state have their starting point and hence also their focal point."[149] This concentration in one hand has a merely symbolic significance. In principle, there could be different persons who assume the role of starting point for different functions. But at no time can a corporate body step into that role. Decisions can be reached by a corporate body in the manner expounded earlier.[150] When all the

---

146. [Literally, "the state yearns for a unified top."]

147. [*Fiat* is Latin for "let it be done." See Stein's discussion of the *fiat* in CWES 7.]

148. See Jellinek, *Allgemeine Staatslehre,* p. 666. [See note 34, above.]

149. [See Jellinek, *Allgemeine Staatslehre,* p.683.]

150. [Stein must intend some difference between a "starting point" (*Auslaufspunkt*) and a "decision" (*Beschluß*); otherwise the last two sentences would be contradictory.]

state's actions depend on the decisions of a corporate body, the latter can count as a "state government" and you can speak of collegial leadership of the state.

The performance of the actions decided upon can also be collective, so that the roles are distributed among the members of the governing committee and accordingly among a series of subordinate agencies. But regardless of the fact that each initiates *his* share of the action with his own "fiat!" the *overall* action has to be set in motion by one individual.[151] It's all the same, whether this is now taken over by a controlling personality on her own initiative, or whether someone is designated in each single case as the performing agent (in this special sense), or whether for each civil function it's provided once and for all who takes over the initiative.

We've still got the question of whether a distinction mentioned earlier makes any viable sense. This was the distinction between "psychological" and "juridical" formations of the will, and correspondingly of a psychological person or (as it's usually said) a physical person. We saw how a community act of willing was differentiated from an individual one. The former is possible only thanks to the participation of individual acts of willing; but just because of that, you can't say it would have a reality inferior to theirs or that it would not be a psychological datum while they would. Certainly there's a possible sense adhering to the expression "juridical reality," namely, the distinctive being of legal objectivities that arise out of legally operative acts (like a demand, an obligation, a contract) and the "being in effect" of positive law.

This being is altogether different from that of the acts from which it arises and, further, also from the being of any acts that are fulfilled subsequently *according to* laws in effect. What this last has to signify is yet to be explained. [The phrase] "juridically formed willing" can present nothing other than an act of willing that is performed in a legally prescribed modality (for example, the vote of a chamber whose proceedings are constitutionally

---

151. [Literally, "must be brought into rolling." This is a pun on "roles," above. The German spelling is the same.]

stipulated). Such an act of willing is to be regarded as having just as much "psychological reality"[152] as some other act that has not been guided by prescribed norms as it was running its course. Out of the fabric of the acts themselves, you've got to show how it is that norms are able to exert an influence over the way the acts transpire.

Yet this is not the case with corporate acts right off, but surely with individual acts, and only because of that with the former as well. You can make it a rule never to make a decision without "deliberating," which means without weighing the pros and cons. And then when you get into a spot where you are to make a decision, *referring back to* that resolve you engage in deliberation, on the basis of which the decision is then accomplished. Such control is possible only as far as the sphere of freedom reaches. You can try to repress joy and sorrow, hope and fear, and the like on the basis of a resolve as soon as they arise—because repression itself belongs to the sphere of freedom. You can also, in keeping with a norm, make up your mind to do something in combination with these feelings—but you can't dictate how they will run their course.[153] Actions, by contrast, can be directed so and so however you please, and therefore according to an established plan. And because this holds true for individual acts, the corporate acts that they help to build up can also be brought into a steady form. We can distinguish in this way between naive and as it were rationalized performances of the will (both in the case of individuals and with corporate bodies).

Does it make sense to ascribe any particular "juridical reality" to such rationalized performances of will? This should be addressed only in connection with the question of the "juridical

---

152. [Literally, "psychic reality." The adjective *psychisch* is different from the one translated the same way in the preceding paragraph, *psychologisch*. Stein usually uses *psychisch* in a technical sense, translated "sentient" or "sensate" elsewhere. See CWES 7.]

153. [Literally, "you can't prescribe for them their positive course." In other words, emotions cannot be voluntarily produced or banished, but they can be managed.]

person." On this concept, Bernatzik[154] had the following to say, with reference to Gerber's "Fundamentals of Civil Law," where the concept was first discussed in that sense: "now for us it coincides with the concept of *legal competence,*" that is, the ability to be a carrier of a *subjective right.*[155]

What is a subjective right? And what does it mean to be the carrier of such a right? We must start to get some clarity for ourselves about this. As the possessor of a competence, I have the right to use it as I please. This right that I have is not a state of affairs subsisting on its own, like those "rights" that in their totality make up the repertoire of pure law. But neither is it an operative regulation of the kind that make up any positive law. Thus there's "right" in yet a third sense. We accept the term "subjective right" for this because it's essential to this right that it be in the possession of a subject. But on what grounds is it also to be designated as *right?* Because in principle it owes its origin

---

154. Edmund Bernatzik, "Kritische Studien über den Begriff der juristischen Person und über die juridische Persönlichkeit der Behörden insbesondere," *Archiv für öffentliches Recht* 5 (1890), pp. 169-318; [reprint 1996 by Springer-Verlag as vol. 113 of Forschung aus Staat und Recht. Stein's citation, from p.191 of the 1890 edition, closes the quote incorrectly at the end of the sentence, mistakenly implying that the term "subjective right" (*subjektives Recht*) is used in that place. Bernatzik's work is a technical survey of the development of the concept of "juridical person" in nineteenth-century legal theory; his reference is to Carl Friedrich von Gerber, *Grundzüge des deutschen Staatsrechts,* 3rd. ed., (Leipzig: Bernhard Tauchnitz, 1880). Bernatzik (1854-1919) went on to become a professor at the University of Vienna. He advocated admission of women to higher studies in the law, in a famous essay in 1900. Bernatzik was mentor to the Austrian legal scholar Hans Kelsen, whose influential books of the late 1920s and 1930s bear comparison with this treatise of Stein's.]

155. ["Right" (*Recht*) is the same word in German as "law" earlier in the same sentence. It is "subjective" in the sense that it pertains to a particular subject. "Subjective" here does not suggest that the right exists merely in someone's imagination.]

to an "objective" right, that is, to a state of affairs of pure law or to a determination of positive law; and furthermore, because it belongs to that specific legal objectivity that forms the material for the simple fact of pure law[156] and for the determinations of positive law.[157] When "natural human rights" have been discussed,[158] this talk can have only one sense: that it's right a priori to grant certain subjective rights to human persons. (The rightness of this statement can be left aside here.)

The meaning of subjective right can be made yet more precise, as follows. What authorizes a subject to perform certain acts is [either] the simple fact of right[159] or a legal regulation. This delimits a category of acts whose performance by a subject eligible for them is declared to be right. The subject is also capable of the same acts independently of all operative and subsisting law. But they don't rest "lawfully" with him or form the content of a subjective right except on the basis of an objective right.

The person who has become the holder of a subjective right has acquired through this a new dignity. She herself has entered the realm of specific legal objectivities, and in that sense you can actually accord to her a special "juridical reality." For certain persons, legal norms prescribe the mode of their formation of will; and therefore you can also speak meaningfully of a "juridical will." (Of course, this is not to be set off against the "psychologi-

---

156. [*Reine Rechtsverhalte,* "the simple fact of pure law," evokes an earlier phenomenological discussion; see above, Part I §2.a.]

157. On the theme of legal objectivities, see below, Part II §§3-4.

158. [Stein may be referring to discussions by Bernatzik or Kelsen; see note 154 above. See also p.141 below.]

159. [*Rechtsverhalt,* "the simple fact of right," can also mean "the simple fact that there is law." See note 156, above. The acts in question here are those that belong to the special class of acts that bring legal realities into being.]

cal" will, because it follows from the very fabric of willing as such that as it goes along it can be determined by norms of this kind.)

Now what should be considered as potential holders of subjective rights? First off, individual persons. (In legal terminology they are designated physical persons.) Provided that as free subjects they are capable of performing acts, it also makes sense to concede this to them as a right. On the same grounds, it's also clear that *federations* of persons can be provided with subjective rights. But what if there's no possibility of performing acts on their own? What sense does it make for the positive law[160] to guarantee subjective rights for underage children, for the mentally ill, or even for inanimate formations such as an endowment? This also has to do with the delineation of the realm of acts, and therefore any subjective right is meaningful only with reference to persons who can perform them.

But it is not required that the persons authorized to perform an act are simultaneously the possessors of the corresponding right. They might be authorized to perform only "in the name of" those who do possess the right. The phenomenon of *representation* is the basis for the legal competence of non-personal formations. They can be provided with rights to the extent that it's possible for persons to entrust them with the protection of their rights. Representation itself is a legal relationship to be grounded through objective right. A person who is in a position to perform legally effective acts can appoint a representative for herself, whom she entrusts with the protection of one of her rights or even all of them. In doing this, she does not divest herself of her rights, but merely leaves to another the performance of the acts in question. The other, in that he "takes on" the representation, commits himself to perform any acts as need be, and out of this arises a demand for the representative to do that. Just as on the other side, the transfer of representation gives rise to a right for him to perform these acts as well as a demand that they be

---

160. [Positive law is enacted law: civil statutes that have been put "on the books."]

recognized as legally binding.[161] The representative performs the acts "in the name of" the one represented, and so the latter fulfills them "through him."

If it's a non-personal formation that possesses the right, then the transfer of representation must be dealt with from another angle. Here too, a claim arises out of the representation for the possessor of the right. This entity is no more able to assert this claim itself than to protect its remaining rights. Therefore the claim, too, is assigned to a person who does so in its name. But when any act is performed in the name of the entity by a person who represents it, the act counts as having been performed by the entity through the person. This is how non-personal formations become potential subjects of acts.

How does somebody come into possession of a subjective right? Through pure law or positive law, as we said. For example, pure law certifies that a claim arises from a promise, along with the right for the bearer of the claim to assert the claim. Furthermore, this right can be guaranteed to him by a positive law. The positive law can confer further rights that would not subsist by virtue of pure law: these might include the right of the father to the assets of the children. But in all cases, every subjective right presupposes some kind of right-realizing act through which it comes to life. (Promising and law-making are such acts, in the examples given above.)

The subject of the right-realizing act can in principle be the same person as the possessor of the right. This is so in the case where a person grants herself the (subjective) right to make (positive) law. She herself performs the right-realizing act through which she becomes the possessor of the subjective right.

But does she perform it *in her own name?* Obviously not. Suppose a father claims for himself the right to protect the rights

---

161. There's an obvious distinction here between a subjective right and a demand, in that a right is always directed toward your own behavior, while the demand is in principle addressed to another. But every right is necessarily tied to a demand, and vice versa.

of his children: he does this in the name of what is objectivly right.[162] [In other words, he does it either in the name] of positive law or [in the name] of what is simply the right thing to do, either really or to his way of thinking.[163] The operative or subsisting legal order is then the non-personal formation in whose name that act is performed. This is how it stands in all cases where someone arrogates command authority to himself without simultaneously denying the presence of a law independent of himself and binding upon him.

Thus we still have to examine the case where this qualification no longer applies, and where a greater law-making authority is no longer recognized. As is easily seen, this is the case of the self-positing sovereign authority of the state. Do we have here a subject that claims for itself, in its own name, the right to make law without restriction by any other authority? Certainly not. In that act of self-positing, the civil authority simultaneously defines its sovereign sphere and constitutes the state. To set itself up as civil authority means to posit itself as representative of the state, and that is an act that is performed in the name of the state. Thus the state, this non-personal formation, is the subject to which all subjective rights refer, as to their ultimate possessor, insofar as they are sources of positive law.

Why then would the concept of the "juridical person" have

---

162. [*Im Namen des objektiven Rechts*, "in the name of what is objectively right," is literally "in the name of objective right/law." Context governs the choice of either "right" or "law" to translate *Recht*.]

163. [*Im Namen . . . eines wirklichen oder vermeintlichen reinen Rechtsverhaltnis*, "in the name . . . of what is simply the right thing to do, either really or to his way of thinking," is literally "in the name . . . of a real or putative pure law condition." Grammatically, Stein indicates here that "what is objectively right" includes two categories: "positive law," i.e., laws that have been properly enacted at some point in time, and pure law/right (*Recht*). Pure law or right simply is. These concepts were introduced above; see p.38. See also note 110.]

been formulated? As we try to discover the sense of this, we must proceed on the basis of the foregoing analysis of subjective right. Obviously, what we want to get at with this concept are the carriers of subjective rights. Starting from the fact that non-personal formations can be carriers of rights, let's try to understand the distinction between juridical persons and physical persons, even if we can't go along with that distinction—in its usual mode. To use the term "person" for everything that is a possessor of rights signifies an expansion of that concept beyond the range of what person is, in the strict sense of the word. This expansion is justified by the fact that all possessors of rights that are not real live persons still are founded upon real live persons in some modality or other, and thanks to this founding relationship, they share with them the ability to perform free acts. With that reservation, we'll accept the term.

The separation into physical persons and juridical persons goes awry if—as often happens—the "physical" persons, meaning individual persons, who alone are real live persons in the full sense, are excluded from the range of juridical persons. The distinction is justified provided that the individual persons as well as the non-personal formations under consideration are on their own merely *capable* of becoming juridical persons but don't become so except through endowment with subjective rights.[164]

We agree with Bernatzik when he rejects the ability to will as the criterion for defining the realm of juridical persons.[165] The ability to will—understood to entail the ability to perform free acts—merely authorizes the acquisition of juridical personality,

---

164. [In other words, the concept of "juridical person" includes a component that is not necessarily included in the concept "physical person": to be in actual possession of "subjective rights," defined as entitlements to press claims arising from promises, commitments, and the like. All persons have rights. But a person doesn't acquire subjective rights unless and until those rights are realized through a social act.]

165. [See Bernatzik, "Kritische Studien," pp. 193-219; see note 154 above.]

but does not yet guarantee its possession. On the other hand, the ability to will—understood as an ability to perform acts *on your own*—is by no means a *conditio sine qua non*[166] for possessing rights. But agreeing with this critique doesn't mean we recognize the theory that Bernatzik opposes to "the dogma of the will." According to [Bernatzik's own] theory, the unity of the juridical person would be delineated through a purpose or even a system of purposes that certain rights serve. "The subject of a right . . . is the carrier of a human purpose which the prevailing legal order recognizes as an end in itself by conferring legal power upon the willing that is necessary for its own realization."[167] For us, the concept of subjective right has been defined in such a way that it is not tied to the idea of purpose. In our view, a right authorizes you to perform certain acts. But whether or not those acts serve a definite purpose is not of importance in principle. And the prevailing legal order could confer rights without worrying if the *motive* for conferring a right is the recognition of a purpose whose advancement it tends to support, even if it may be so as a rule.

So by no means is there any need to define the *unity* of the juridical person through a purpose or a system of purposes, because what becomes a person through endowment with subjective juridical rights in most cases already possesses a unity regardless of that and therefore is capable on its own of pulling together into a unity the manifold of rights that may be independent of each other.[168] This is entirely obvious with the individual

---

166. [*Conditio sine qua non* is Latin for "condition without which not," or "necessary condition."]

167. See Bernatzik, "Kritische Studien," p. 233. [One word was mis-copied in Stein's citation: *notwendigen* instead of *erforderlichen* in the original. Both terms mean "necessary." Stein indicates that she does not accept the view that rights arise from the fact that human beings are ends in themselves, in the Kantian sense.]

168. [For the phenomenologists, "unity" signifies self-identical subsistence. Stein argues that a juridical person (for example, a corporation) is already the "something" that it is before it takes on subjective rights. The entity is not a mere bundle of different rights.]

person, and you'd have to be totally tangled up in hollow verbal definitions to overlook the fact that personhood indicates a substantial sense independent of the whole sphere of law and presupposed for it.

Yet even the non-personal formations that come under consideration as having rights generally possess their unity entirely independently of any purpose served by the rights that they acquire. Take a family, for example. In no way can it be said that the family is a unity in regard to a purpose, or that the rights with which the family as a unity is endowed and to which it owes its character as a juridical person are granted in the service of the purpose that is founding the unity of the family. Certainly there are also "federations with a purpose," that is, federations into which persons have joined together solely for achieving a purpose, and which aspire to and receive their rights purely in the interest of their purpose. And as a possible special case, it is to be conceded that juridical persons are created on the part of the law-making and right-granting authority specifically for the sake of a certain purpose, and therefore owe their existence and their unity to that purpose and to the rights that were granted to them for its sake. For example, if a panel of jurors is called up, then through that constituting act the whole set of persons is authorized for common performance of certain specifically circumscribed acts. A unity is created that did not subsist before.

Now it's a very controversial question whether councils that generally fall under this type are to be regarded as juridical persons. Bernatzik thinks: "Where it's only a question of a common legal *duty,* the category of juridical person makes no intelligible sense. Here there is neither the possibility of a common control of the will nor the commonality of one purpose, but only a common *yoking* of the will . . . .[169]" As we have seen,

---

169. Bernatzik, "Kritische Studien," p. 221, note 171. [See note 154, above. *Willensherrschaft,* "control of the will," and *Willensgebundenheit,* "yoking of the will," use the possessive construction in contrasting senses. The former connotes a single will in an active role and shared by all. The latter connotes many wills in a passive role of being reined in and taken over.]

neither the element of control of the will nor the purpose is constitutive for the juridical person, but only the element of subjective right. And now the most amazing correlation obtains, that there's no legal yoking at all without a legal entitlement essentially tied to it. This has already impressed itself upon us repeatedly, but we haven't yet formulated it as a general principle. For example, we saw that the responsibility of a representative to look after the rights of another corresponds with the right of performing acts in the name of the other and the claim for recognition of those acts as proceeding from the one represented. Thus the right to be recognized as citizens corresponds to the duties of the citizens, and a *collective* entitlement also corresponds to every *collective* responsibility of a plurality of persons (which is entirely different from an *equal* responsibility of the single individuals).

As a consequence of these remarks, it can be claimed that besides the state, the councils representing it and even the citizens singly are juridical persons. This will look like an absurdity only to someone for whom the difference between real live and juridical personhood has not become clear. If you substitute the concept of the real live (that is, the individual) person for that of the juridical person, you must certainly be amazed how it then would be possible for one person to contain a multiplicity of persons. But there's no difficulty to be found in the notion that a series of individual persons and a formation that is founded on this multiplicity of individual persons can each in itself be a carrier of rights—in the mode that the individual persons perform acts sometimes on their own and sometimes in the name of the whole formation. And it's not just merely possible, but also necessary, for anyone who exercises rights in the name of a juridical person to be simultaneously the carrier of a right of her own, that is, to be a juridical person herself.

*

The view of the juridical person presented in the text [above], and its significance for the relevant definition of the concept of state, are suggested in E. Albrecht's well known review of Maurenbrecher's *Grundsatzen des heutigen deutschen Staats-*

rechts.[170] He conceives of the state—entirely in our sense—not as an alliance of human beings for the sake of individual purposes, but rather:

> as an institution standing above the individuals that is first of all devoted to purposes that in no way form merely the sum of individual interests of the ruler and his subjects, but rather form a higher general collective interest, from which is mediated to the state its nourishment, advancement, and direction. Consequently the life of the individual (of ruler and subjects) divides into two parts, the one, in which he is authorized or obliged for the sake of that generality, in the name and the service of the state, as the head or as a member of the state, the other in which he as an independent individual has rights for his own sake or obligations for the sake of another. In that we consequently deny the individual all independent juridical personhood (the being-entitled for his own sake) in connection with the first area, we are necessarily led to the conclusion that the personality who rules, acts, and has rights in that area is to be ascribed to the state, and *the latter is to be thought of as a juridical person.* And this, rightly understood, has relevance for the basic formulation of that view of the state that he has called the true civil law view.

Albrecht himself emphasizes that the clarification of the concept of juridical person that would be needed for a deeper grounding of this view is still something to be desired.

---

170. [This paragraph is a lengthy footnote in the German original. Stein quotes the reviewer's synopsis rather than quoting Maurenbrecher directly. The work reviewed is Romeo Maurenbrecher, *Grundsatzen des heutigen deutschen Staatsrechts* (Frankfurt am Main: Verlag von Franz Varrentrapp, 1837). The review appears in the] *Göttingische Gelehrte Anzeigen* of September 21 and 23, 1837 [(no. 150-1, pp. 1489-1504, and no. 152, pp. 1508-15). The citation is taken from] p.1492.

g) Law and state in the Middle Ages

The view of law and state that was advocated here makes a sharp distinction between pure law, which subsists all by itself, and posited law, which requires the state as its ultimate source. It also insists that the state is unrestricted in its law-making. [But] this view seems not to be able to take into account certain facts of historical life. For example, how would it let us understand the concept of "good old law" and medieval legal practices?[171] According to that concept, law that has been in effect since time immemorial is unalterable; and it's permissible to make new law only if it derives from the old law and shows itself to be a consequence of the old law, or if you can show that the new law abolishes habitual injustice and restores the older law.

To my way of thinking, this medieval view is based on the idea of *pure* law. The idea of pure law is not yet separated from the idea of morality, and apart from the latter is interpreted falsely (by being tied to time). It's absurd to suppose that the fact of having been made long ago should require unalterability.[172] On the contrary, you assume that what is right (in a material sense) always holds steady, so you think that the old law ought not to be

---

171. See F. Kern, "Recht und Verfassung im Mittelalter," *Historische Zeitschrift* 24/1. [The reference is obscure. Stein may have confused her notes on an article by Fritz Kern in the *Historische Zeitschrift* of 1919 with a review of Georg Ludwig von Maurer, *Zur Geschichte der Städtverfassung im Mittelalter* (Erlangen, 1869) by C. Hegel in *Historische Zeitschrift* 24/1 (1870) pp. 1-21. See Fritz Kern, "Law and Constitution in the Middle Ages," *Kingship and Law in the Middle Ages,* trans. Stanley B. Chimes (Oxford: Basil Blackwell, 1939, 1956).]

172. [In other words, if a law is unalterable, then it is so for some reason other than having been posited at a point in time that just happens to be very long ago. Stein suggests that such law is unalterable because is has no temporal point of origin at all. Pure law, "right versus wrong as such," does not change and does not go in or out of existence. See p.38, above.]

tampered with.[173] The idea of law-making[174] and of positive law, which intrinsically can deviate from pure law, then does not apply at all. The law (the pure law materially implemented) is discovered and becomes articulated, and in regard to it there is only the one task: to cherish it.

The idea of one law-making authority also becomes untenable along with the idea of the positive law. The monarch, who appears as supreme head of the medieval commonwealth, is [viewed as] not the source of the law but the commissioned guardian of the law. But guarding the law is incumbent upon everyone else besides him, too—indeed, this is a moral duty, not a function of the civil law—and if the ruler transgresses against it, then the law must be protected against him.

Where the idea of the positive law is lacking, the idea of the state cannot be grasped either—as may be deduced from our exposition. The patrimonial view sees the territory of the state as the property of the ruler and the political functions that he exercises as so-called proprietary rights that can be conferred with the property itself. But this view does not extend to the state, as a formation in its own right, independent of the land area as well as the persons who occupy its positions. Nor does our idea of a civil authority that represents the state as a whole correspond to the king chosen as leader of an ethnic or tribal community in their

---

173. [Literally, "so it is thoroughly conceivable that the old law should not be touched." The issue here is to identify the reason why. Mere age is not a good reason, Stein says. We tacitly acknowledge something that does not change with time; this is what the phenomenologists call "pure law."]

174. Only in the mode of *divine* law-making can the idea maintain itself, inasmuch as the pure law is regarded as a part of the divine arrangement of the world. (See Kern, "Law and Constitution.") [See note 169, above. Stein cites p. 5 of the German edition.] *Whether* the pure law admits of such a meaning won't be discussed here. *Even* with that meaning, pure law remains unassailable with respect to "human statutes," especially with respect to the regulations of a civil authority.

enterprises, or as the most capable guardian of the law—excelling purely as a person in a community of persons.

Suppose we try taking the primary datum to be the lack of a full-blown idea of the state, and infer from that the absence of the idea of positive law. When the state is not viewed as a self-regulating community, doesn't the idea of law-making have to become invalid too? In fact, there's no room for positive law when only the peoples, or perhaps a unity comprising many peoples (such as Christendom), are viewed as communities, and when those who rule them are viewed as their leaders, and the institutions that they live by work as an independent order entrusted to their custody.

Yet it would be wrong to speak of the priority of an idea or of what it encompasses. As already emphasized above, it's neither state *before* law nor vice versa; rather, as to the idea, they belong inseparably together. You can't say that the one must be grasped *first* so that the other can be grasped. In fact, either idea can be grasped first just as easily, with the other following as a consequence. (How this might have been posed in the Middle Ages is therefore a historical question, not a philosophical one.) And in fact the one or the other idea can also be *realized* first: a positive law that has no civil authority behind it yet—a state that has not yet engaged in law-making.

Of course it would be wrong to infer from the lack of a proper comprehension of state and law that there also could not have been the corresponding concrete patterns in the Middle Ages. Thus precisely because the idea of law was oriented toward the right[175] in a material sense (that is, toward that which is moral) it's quite possible that to a large extent, law-making was performed without anyone's having a clear idea that what they were doing was making law. However, with every decree of the ruler the query can be put, upon which right is it based. He must be ready to prove that he had a subjective right to perform such an act. There are subjective rights only on the basis of pure law, which

---

175. [One word, *Recht,* translates as "law" and "right"; the choice depends on the context.]

means they must either figure into the content of a relationship of pure law or be shown to obtain through an analytical inference from a relationship of pure law. (Let's consider this pure law relation: a claim arises from a promise. You can analytically infer from this that when A has made a promise to B, B possesses a claim.) The sense of justice of the people or even of a lone human being can protest against an action of government, and as a result the legitimacy of that action can be disputed. In principle that is always possible, according to the medieval view. But without a doubt, lots of law-making for which a legal basis (in the sense of pure law) was lacking actually transpired uncontested.

Accordingly, wherever political functions are exercised, the state is present as a reality (even if perhaps understood as under development), without any need for the idea of the state to be formulated. This still does not prevent the prevailing view of state and law from influencing the configuration of the concrete pattern.[176] Thus the thought of the conferability of political functions, as it came to be expressed in feudalism, could lead to the emergence of new dominions by way of conferral at the expense of the original civil authority, threatening to dissolve the state to which they owed their existence. On the other hand, the idea of legal protection against the prevailing civil authority could become the basis for placing subordinate persons and bodies in possession of political functions and thus giving rise to a change in the civil constitution.

h) The idea of legal protection

However, the idea of legal protection still must be discussed under another viewpoint entirely. So far we've approached it only from the idea of pure law. But there's a way to get at it from positive law as well. Indeed, we started out by stressing that the preservation of the positive law is just as much the business of the law-making authority as is the making of that law. But we found besides that for law to *be in effect*, it must be not merely made but

---

176. See below, Part I §3.h.

also recognized on the part of those for whom it is made. Law is obliged on both sides and, for its part, obliges on both sides.

Whoever makes a law commits himself thereby to hold himself to the law that he has made. (It's quite in keeping with this, that his person is not involved in the content of his regulations or expressly excluded either.) For anyone who is affected by a law and recognizes it, the claim arises from this that he will proceed according to that law. If persons in a sovereign territory break a law that's in effect there, it's up to the civil authority to "protect" the law against them. But what if the law is broken by those who occupy [positions of] civil authority? Obviously there has to be a "legal protection" against them too.

Notice here: if such a breach of the law occurs, it's not the state that breaks the law but the person who represents the state. The life of the state is limited to law-making and to actions with a legal basis.[177] Every breach of the law is to be regarded as a disruption of the life of the state. From this it must be understood that positions in the state are occupied by persons who are nothing but its representatives. Sometimes when they are supposed to be acting as representatives they allow themselves to be determined by motives and pushed into actions that are alien to the state. Against such eventualities there must be a remedy purely from the standpoint of the state. This is at the same time the perspective from which the desire for "civil rights" takes on its rational sense.[178] This demand is absurd [as a demand] in opposition to the state, because what counts as civil rights from the standpoint of positive law presupposes the demand for maintenance of the operative law and is just as important as the maintenance of the state itself. However, it does make good sense [to demand civil rights] in opposition to those who may hold civil authority at any

---

177. We're considering it here in itself, and disregarding external activities. We're about to discuss [below] how matters stand with "breaches of law" in the transactions between states.

178. [*Bürgerrechten,* "civil rights," is literally "citizens' rights." In the next sentence Stein is able to link civil rights to the state because the concept of citizenship entails the concept of the state.]

given time and their possible deviations from the intentions of the state.[179]

Seen from the side of the state, the only possible safeguard against infringements of this kind is to arrange for a control on the leadership of the state and its agencies through civil regulations. Again, with this you still leave open [the question of] to whom or to what this control would be assigned: to an authority unto itself, or to the individual citizens in their entirety. Where no such safeguard is arranged by statute, there again any breach of the law by those who are ruling can be answered only by another breach of the law—from the side of the subjects or subordinate agencies—maybe with a refusal of compliance in opposition to an unlawful ordinance. The substance of the state is undoubtedly shaken by such a reactive breach of the law just as it is by that which brings it on.

Therefore, you can't talk about a "right of revolution" if you take "right" in the strict sense.[180] (We don't have to investigate here how this would apply to the "moral law.") However, rebellion against the subsisting civil order and struggle toward a new one can be entirely within the sense of state, insofar as through this you're working toward a condition in which the state would be better secured against breaches of the law. Thus the idea of legal protection in the second meaning—the one oriented to positive law—could become the starting point for founding a "sharing of powers" and the transference of political functions to the citizens, and for reorganizing concrete civil patterns along this line.

---

179. [Stein's argument is that a violation of civil rights by the state itself would be a contradiction in terms.]

180. [Or, "if you take 'law' in the strict sense." Because "right" and "law" are the same word in German (*Recht*), the concepts are very closely linked. Stein may have in view the 1918 November Revolution and the founding of the Weimar Republic. Her argument applies equally well to any instance of civil disobedience leading to rehabilitation of the state, not to its dissolution.]

i) The legal foundations for transactions between states

In stipulating the relation between state and law, we have left out of consideration the relationships of states to one another —apart from occasional remarks. Can transactions between states be brought into the picture without undermining the assertion that the life of the state is limited to law-making and actions with a legal basis? The history of the world seems to teach us that in their external activity, states do not abide by any legal foundation but are guided only or at least mainly by the necessities of life and the lust for power. In contrast to that is the conviction that an international law obtains and is binding for transactions among states. And now it will be our task to examine what is contained in this *idea of international law.*[181]

Let's orient ourselves once more by our distinction between pure law and positive law. Hugo Grotius explains [it] as *ius gentium: quod gentium omnium aut multarum voluntate vim accepit,*[182] but adds that only the *natural law* would be binding for all peoples. Therefore—since according to our view the "natural law" is merely an erroneous interpretation of pure law—in the repertoire of international law we would have to distinguish between statements of pure law and agreements by the discrete states about the modalities of their reciprocal transactions. In fact, if a state is accused of a breach of international law, you usually hear that it has done something "against which the sense of justice rebels."[183] But the sense of justice speaks only for that which is

---

181. [*Völkerrecht,* "international law," is literally "law of peoples."]

182. *De iure belli et pacis* L. I, cap. I, 14. [Hugo Grotius (1583-1646), late Renaissance legal scholar, was learned in theology and the humanities. The Latin phrase means "law of peoples, receiving its force from the will of all or many peoples."]

183. [*Rechtsgefühl,* "sense of justice," is literally "feeling of right" or "feeling of law." Feelings would be an indicator of pure law, but not of positive law, which comprises laws that have been enacted at some time and place.]

right in a material sense—and in this case, that means pure law. The content of a positive law need not—according to the idea of positive law—be right in a material sense. Thus a sense of justice can't tell you what is in accord with the regulations of a positive law and what contradicts them. For example, when breaking a treaty is designated as a violation of international law, in no way is it required that the content of the treaty be right in the material sense. Nevertheless from the standpoint of pure law you're dealing with a breach of the law. Independently of all [law-] making, then, it is right that treaties should be kept (regardless of their content), and the sense of justice rebels against the breach of the treaty as such.

On the other hand, as for the content of agreements between states, you're going to have to say that they need to be right only in a *formal* sense—which means as a norm that's in effect merely by virtue of right-positing.[184] (Don't be confused by the fact that you find the form and content juxtaposed here twice, and they switch places: the form of the treaty goes into the content of the material right, while the content of the treaty deserves to be called right only in a formal sense of right.) But now there's a new difficulty to mention: according to our exposition, the ideas "state" and "positive law" reciprocally demand each other. Positive law is "posited" law, and it needs an authority standing behind it which does the law-making.

With international law (in the sense now of regulations valid for transactions between states), where do we have a civil

----

184. [*Rechtsetzung,* "right-positing," is the same term translated elsewhere as "law-making." Thanks to the ambiguity of *Recht* in German, *Rechtsetzung* can refer to any instance when a right or a law is brought into being where none existed before, as happens when a treaty is made. The distinction between formal and material ethics was discussed by Max Scheler in a work that impressed Stein deeply during her student years, *Formalism in Ethics and Non-Formal Ethics of Values.* See note 58, above. "Formalism" in this context refers to a Kantian, transcendental approach to the determination of right and wrong. The phenomenologists generally were critical of it.]

authority in which to vest the law-making? Grotius said that international law acquires its validity through the will of the peoples. For consistency here we have to replace "peoples" with "states"—even the term *Völkerrecht*[185] is inadequate to what it should express. Therefore the international legal regulations would be regarded as agreements between states. Neither "agreement" nor "regulation" correctly expresses the character of the principles of international law, however. This can't be about mere arrangements—that is, airing opinions and stating intentions of how you propose to behave yourself—because there's no sense of "right" in which arrangements have binding power. Even straightforward treaties apparently have to be ruled out, because *sensu stricto*[186] they have "validity" only insofar as it's guaranteed by regulation of a positive law.

To put it plainly: If the substance of international law—to the extent that it does not have a pure-law character—is reduced to treaties, then it is not to be regarded as positive law. Somebody might say, and this would have to be the opinion of Grotius, that a plurality of states could *collectively* lay down regulations that would be binding upon them all. Then we would have one corporate body, assembled out of the representatives of the single states, that would claim to make binding law for the collectivity of the participating states. Such a claim can be made only in the name of, or at least on the ground of, the decision of one state. Accordingly, the following possibilities obtain. Either that corporate body constitutes itself as a sovereign civil authority —thereby destroying the single states; or on the authorization of one of the single states it appoints itself a superordinate authority—which would have the same consequence. Or else the body derives its mandate from the single states. Then the whole situation looks different.

No state has the right to issue regulations through its representative for other states. If that corporate body charged with

185. [*Völkerrecht* is literally "law of peoples." It is the usual term for "international law."]

186. [*Sensu stricto* is Latin for "in the strict sense."]

setting standards for transactions between states is deemed to be authorized by the single states, then it doesn't have the potentiality of enacting collective regulations for all participating states. The persons belonging to it can only discuss and decide collectively what each state singly should regulate for its own state. Discussion and decision are matters for the corporate body. Conversely, regulations are a matter for the state on its own. Through them, each state binds only its own state.

In place of international law with validity over and above the state, then, you get a repertoire of similar regulations in the positive law of the single states. This is in fact the only possible way to have a standardization in positive law of transactions among a plurality of commonwealths that is compatible with their existence as *states*. For a state to transgress such regulations of "international law" would mean that it broke its own law, and that would be absurd since the state is the law-maker here as always.[187] With these as with all other regulations, the state retains the freedom to suspend them all by itself, on its own, without the participation of those states with which it collectively decided to issue them. For a decision has no legally binding power. To dissociate itself from a decision may be unwise and might be immoral [of the state, but] in no sense is it a breach of the law.

Here's another possibility. Suppose that a state, through a regulation, suspends a treaty that it has concluded. The claim of the other party that concluded the treaty is then not *canceled* (as is the case according to pure law under certain stipulations —perhaps if it's a question of certain delimited performances and they are totally accomplished), rather, it is annihilated. You've got here an annihilation of pure law (just as happens many times within the life of the state when it wouldn't occur to anyone to mention a breach of law—for example, in all cases where a demand that obtains according to pure law is declared null and

---

187. [Literally, "that would be senseless in comparison with this and all other law-making by the state." Stein holds that it is impossible in principle for the state itself to break the law, although persons who are state officials can and sometimes do break the law.]

void by a regulation of positive law). This annihilation *can* at the same time be a violation of a moral duty. Again, there's no breach of law, in the sense of positive law.

You could still have some qualms about whether the unilateral suspension of a treaty doesn't allow the treaty-breaking state to interfere in its opponent's sphere of [self-] regulation. Nevertheless, regulatory authority is limited to the areas for which the civil authority has been constituted, as we know, and does not reach into other states. No state can determine that another state should have an obligation to it. It can't go beyond the fact that the other state promises it something and that from that promise arises an obligation for the other state and a claim for itself. If the opponent dissociates itself from the obligation and thereby nullifies claim and commitment, that does not touch the [self-] regulation of a foreign state.

Let's return to the issue of whether the state is legally bound in its external conduct in the same way as when confined to itself. The state has its own extraordinary way of being enclosed within itself,[188] and this closure impresses a distinctive mark upon all its external actions. According to its own proper essence, it is placed on its own and isolated. Of the individual person we occasionally said this: she is just as originarily a community member as she is a lone subject, or, her natural mental posture is to be open to exchanges with others.[189] This communicates itself from the

---

188. [*Insichbeschlossensein*, "way of being enclosed within itself," is a made-up phenomenological term. It connotes at once the territorial and political borders of the state, the quality of life within the state, the concept of the state as a complete entity, and the way the state is perceived to be a stable unity amid the flux of its multiple manifestations to consciousness. But see below, p.101, where this view is apparently contradicted.]

189. [Although this has not been so succinctly stated until this point in the treatise, these maxims nicely sum up Stein's discussions in an earlier treatise, "Individual and Community," in CWES 7. By contrast, the self-sufficiency of the state was argued by the Idealist philosopher J.G. Fichte, mentioned below in Part II. See note 329.]

individual person to the communities into which she enters, perhaps to a people. It's even natural for peoples to be opened for others, to receive impressions from each other, and to allow themselves to be regulated in their behavior through them.

This does not hold true for states. They are *literally* "sufficient unto themselves" and their life is a closed circle. If they activate themselves toward the outside, it happens only in the interest of the inner life and not from "external impressions." For example, if the state does not have enough room to maintain its "autarchy," then it takes steps to broaden its sovereign territory. In that, it goes beyond itself. But as soon as the annexation of the area that it needed has occurred, the state closes itself up again. That external action can be combined with interference in the sovereign territory of a foreign state. Then it is in fact a breach of law, that is, a *violation of foreign law.* (An action is also [potentially] an interference with foreign sovereignty when the "international forms" are maintained. A war formally declared is just as much an interference as is an incursion into a foreign area without a declaration of war.)

When we said that the state is permanently bound by the law, that law would be solely its *own* law. To be bound by a foreign law would mean the suspension of its character of being a state. (Of course, foreign law always connotes *positive* law. Pure law remains on the sidelines here entirely.) As soon as the state goes beyond itself, it enters an area that is empty of law for it. Its *own* law is not operative there—as long as the state has not annexed the area—and a foreign law has no significance for the state. Strictly speaking, you can't say that *the state* commits a breach of the law. That only makes sense in regard to a law that you're obliged to keep.

Yet *law is broken* by what the state does. States are rigid formations. If they lie hard up against one another, then when one moves the others are jostled too. As a result, after the push and the jostling they either return to the old circumstances or one is displaced from at least a part of its territory.[190] In every case, the motion is always only a stage on the way to the tranquility that befits the state—a transitory stage in which the state is not entirely itself.

For the time being, we've considered only one possible kind of external activity. Besides military activity there's peaceful activity to consider, as well as other modes of military activity. What if a state is entangled in military operations not by an urge for expansion or defense, but perhaps by outrage over a breach of law, or fidelity to an ally, or something like that? Yet here it seems to be external impressions that are the determining [factor]. The state seems to stand in immediate contact with other states, and its behavior seems to be motivated by their behavior. Nevertheless, such a view rests upon an illusion. That which receives impressions from someone else's behavior and reacts with attitudes like indignation, outrage, frenzy, and so forth is not the state but the community of the people that it encompasses, or even only a certain group within the people's community. They can in this way be stirred to their souls,[191] which the state can't be at all, and on that basis they can be pushed into actions along certain lines.

The action itself, meaning specifically the action of realization, falls within the realm of the state. The state can permit persons within its sovereign territory to undertake an external action on their own initiative (perhaps to participate in a foreign war as volunteers). But it is placed entirely within the state's discretion whether it wishes to allow it or stop it—or ultimately

---

190. The spatial images that had to be resorted to here are supposed to be no more than metaphors. If the "displacement" is to be understood factually as well, then in principle there's no necessity to it. See below, Part I §3.f.

191. [*Seelisch aufgewühlt,* "stirred to their souls," is literally "agitated soulishly." This phrase connotes deep feeling but does not suggest any specifically religious capacity.]

make the cause its own. The state can, on the basis of the agitation of the people, pave the way for a state action. And it's in keeping with the sense of state if the agitation of the people—left to itself—threatens to shake up the substance of the state. But then again it's clear that what determines the outer behavior of the state is its inner life, not external impressions. What foreign states do or tolerate doesn't make any difference to the state as long as the state itself is not inwardly affected by it. And if the responsible leaders let themselves be determined to stage a state action by such motives [that are] alien to the state, then their behavior does not conform to the sense of state.

k) Delimitation of the proxy power of state representatives by the sense of state[192]

A question emerges at this point. Do we have any right not to allow acts performed by representatives of the state in its name to count as the state's acts, just because they do not conform to its sense? Reinach, in his discussion of the problem of representation,[193] emphasizes that these two things are to be thoroughly distinguished: to do transactions in the sense of somebody and to do them as his representative. If a person appoints another as her representative, then she brings forth in him the legal can-do[194] belonging essentially to her as a person (the possibility of performing acts with legal consequences) once again. And provided this occurs without limitation, *every* such act has binding power for the one represented. Any limitation of the acts—maybe to such as are in the sense of the one represented—can be

---

192. [Section k comes immediately after section i. In traditional academic style, lists did not use the letter j since j was merely how the letter i was written when it appeared at the beginning of a word.]

193. See Reinach, "Foundations of Civil Law," pp. 275 ff. [See note 78 above and Part I §2.a.]

194. [*Können*, "can-do," was discussed by Stein in the treatise "Sentient Causality," CWES 7: 97.]

achieved only through special conditions [given] with the giving over of the proxy.

On the other hand, it's certain that no person can transfer to another the representative performance of acts of which she herself is not capable. If A has the right of usufruct[195] on a business that does not belong to him, then he does not have the right to transfer the business to another as a possession. And if he names B as his representative, the transfer of proxy does not confer upon B the possibility of selling or giving away that business. *This* limitation on the acts included in the proxy power is not tied to any special conditions when it was given.

Acts that the state is not able to perform itself cannot be performed in the name of the state either. This is ambiguous, of course. Because we surely know that the state cannot perform acts at all except through representatives. But *which* acts can in principle be performed in the name of the state [is something] that will be stipulated by the *sense* of state. It would be absurd to "forgive" a criminal in the name of the state. On the contrary, it makes perfect sense to excuse him from punishment.

"In keeping with the sense of" is altogether different from "in the sense of."[196] What is not in keeping with the sense of the one

---

195. [*Nutzungsrecht*, "right of usufruct," is a legal term for the profitable use of something that is not owned outright; for example, the right to consume crops growing on land that belongs to someone else, or the right to dividends earned by someone else's stock.]

196. [The first of the two phrases is a phenomenological formulation. *Dem Sinne gemäß*, "in keeping with the sense of," uses the term "sense" to indicate the very idea of something, its essence correctly understood. The second of the two phrases uses the term "sense" in an ordinary colloquial expression. *Im Sinne von*, "in the sense of," refers to agreement with someone else's opinion or fidelity to someone else's wishes. The key difference between the two phrases is that the first refers to an objective and absolute meaning, while the second refers to intentions that are contingent upon someone's particular preferences. "State" as such has an objective, absolute meaning for Stein, prior to any agenda that might be adopted by a particular state.]

represented cannot be considered to be issuing from him or it. Statesmen do many things "in the name of the state" that have no sense in the name of the state, but this implies nothing against that intuitive connection. It is entirely possible for such acts to be allotted the same efficacy in practice as though they had issued from the state: the citizens comply with orders from civic leaders which are given without sanction by any law, never suspecting that in this case they are obeying not the state but the individual person of its representative.

We still want to clear up that discrepancy in the non-warlike external actions of the state. Looking after the rights of its citizens abroad is entirely in conformity with the sense of state. If the state were to abandon them to the caprice of foreign states, it would be consenting to an intervention in its sovereign sphere. It likewise makes sense when the state, in the interest of its economic life, concludes treaties for transactions and deliveries (just as it makes sense when the state intervenes domestically to regulate economic life). On the other hand, pursuing economic enterprises of whatever kind as an end in itself does not conform to the sense of state. Where a civic leader does that, he's exploiting his position as representative to serve his own private preferences, even if he lets the earnings flow into the public treasury without taking a cut.

It's no different with enterprises of other kinds: art collections, scientific expeditions, and the like. None of that makes any sense as an end in itself for the state. The state is *a master*, and as the master[197] it can concern itself with everything that its citizens are doing in the areas named and can it can give them relevant instructions. But the state itself is not an entrepreneur, a scientific explorer, an art-lover, or anything like that. Everything the state does is done under the motto: to be master in its own area. That covers everything. The state is therefore oriented entirely from within. Everything that it does externally is to be understood only

---

197. [*Herr,* "master," is literally "lord." There is no close English equivalent. Stein means to say that the state is in charge of everything in the ways that she specifies. Compare p.58 above, where "the state behaves like an entrepreneur."]

[as determined] from within itself—as a protection and expansion of its inner life. Whatever is not comprehensible from that central point is none of the state's business; it is the affair of individual persons who represent the state and may be making fraudulent use of their representative position.

l) Summary concerning the fabric of the state

Here is what our investigations yield for the ontic fabric of the state. The state is a social pattern into which free persons are inserted in such a way that one or several of them (or in the extreme case, all of them) govern the others in the name of the whole pattern. (In that extreme case, the sector of sovereignty is formed by the same persons who also exercise control, but only insofar as they don't have representative functions.) Besides the persons who are inserted into it, the sector of sovereignty also includes all the objectivities that play a role in their life, to the extent that those objectivities can be engaged in through a free act. The state's governing function is performed through *commands,* by means of which the state sets into action the persons of its domain, and *regulations,* which stipulate what is supposed to count as law within that domain. Government works, and the state is the state, only for as long as the governing function flows from the state.[198] The state can't be under any other control, but must be sovereign.

The life of the state is entirely taken up with the governing function. The realization of that function, and with it the existence of a concrete political system, is contingent upon finding persons to take on its representation and gaining recognition from those addressed by the claim of control.[199]

---

198. [Literally, "It's a governing function for only as long, and the state is a state for only as long, as the governing function has its flow-out point in the state."]

199. [Literally, "is tied to (the condition) that persons are found who undertake its representation and (the condition) that the control-claim is recognized by those to whom it is addressed."]

Yet that still doesn't settle anything about the *content* of the governing function or about *what* the state commands and regulates. The question is whether and to what extent this can be prescribed by its proper sense. If the function of governing comprises the substance of the state, then the single guiding principle that is suggested for it by its own proper sense is the maintenance of that relation of control. Therefore the state *must* order and regulate what is required for that purpose. It's *permitted to* regulate and order what does not stand in the way of that purpose. It *may not* regulate or order anything that could hinder it.

The third category—commands and regulations that are ruled out by the sense of state—includes all those whose content is likely to jeopardize the recognition of the relation of control: those which could provoke insubordination on the part of the subjects or even aggression on the part of foreign powers against its sovereignty. (For example, that could be commands whose content arouses moral indignation, or that make severe demands upon the capacities of the citizens. But it could also be those that give rise to uncertainty about the firmness of the will to govern.) Conversely, the *obligatory* acts might include the punishment of any insurrection against the civil authority, the defense of the territory against aggression, and the like.

The really problematic area is the [one in between[200]]: the realm of that which is *allowed* by the sense of state. What conventional theories of the state described as the "purpose" or "mission" of the state (such as establishment of a "moral regime," assurance of the free development of the nation, care for the welfare of the people) can have a place only here—if anywhere at all. It is not prescribed for the state by its proper sense that it should place itself at the service of the moral law, or that it must be a "moral regime." As a state, the reign of Satan can be just as perfect as the reign of God. The only question is how the "spirit" of the former or the latter takes over the content of the state regulations and in that way can impress its seal upon the entire

---

200. [Literally, "the third." This is the third category discussed, but it was the second one named above.]

concrete pattern of the state, since the state as such does not prescribe it and has no agency for imparting any [particular] spirit.[201]

We've seen that, precisely because the state abides in the sphere of freedom, it is not self-contained and must receive direction-giving motives for its activity from elsewhere.[202] The motivation is effectuated in the persons who represent the state. What they do on the basis of motives that they experience (motives not experienced by the state itself) has to count as an act of the state, if it's in keeping with the sense of state. If it's contrary to the sense of state, then it merely looks like a state act —even if everything transpires as though you had an act of the state. Then the representatives of the state—maybe in good faith —have preformed a representative act for which they lacked the proxy power.

This always signifies a certain danger for the state. It is at once a *symptom* of the fact that not everything in the state is entirely in order, and can be a *cause* of further disturbances as well. That kind of thing happens in the life of every state, and any state can tolerate a series of such jolts. [But if] too many accumulate, they undermine its existence. That doesn't go for acts that we designated as *allowed* by the sense of state. But this is still not to say that they have to count as genuine state acts. Suppose that an

---

201. [*Geist,* "spirit," can also mean "mind." Stein probably has no theological intention here, but mentions God and Satan (literally, "the satan") only as a rhetorical flourish. The sobering irony of this passage, written about 1921, was not apparent until several decades later when Stein and so many others were put to death under the Nazi regime.]

202. [*In sich unabgeschlossen ist,* "is not self-contained," apparently contradicts what was said above on p.93. The term "motivation" has a technical meaning in phenomenology, discussed at length by Stein in an earlier publication; see CWES 7. Motivation is distinguished from causation, and can be experienced only by entities endowed with minds. This is why the state as such cannot experience motivation.]

administration adopts measures for educational affairs that can neither really nor allegedly serve the state, but also cannot harm the state. Then you've got a use of the state for a purpose alien to itself and, in turn, an expansion of the proxy power beyond the realm covered by its sense.[203] The state can approve such a use, because it remains unharmed by it. That's why we call the acts allowed (from the viewpoint of the state)—but they're not acts *of the state* in the strict sense.

This restriction of the acts to that which is prescribed by the sense of state does not stand in contradiction to what we established earlier: that in principle the state can take charge of the management of all enterprises in its territory. For no action is in principle excluded from being in accordance with the sense of state. It *can* lie within the interest of the state for the youth to be educated in a certain manner: perhaps so that they learn to fit into the state in the right way. Or to be concerned about the material welfare of the citizens: perhaps over their disposition to subordinate themselves to the authority of the state, or even for the sake of its own economic independence.

Let's get back to the question of how a certain "spirit" could take over the content of state acts.[204] It can correspond to the sense of state that its "policy" breathes a certain spirit, that is, seems motivated according to a fixed type. This spirit will always correspond to the ethos of the people forming the sector of sovereignty of the state, because to govern counter to that ethos means to cut the state off from the roots of its existence. Wherever policy departs from what the sense of state prescribes—that means, where policy is composed of acts that are not really acts of state[205]—what is speaking there is merely the spirit that prevails in the representatives of the state. Inasmuch as that spirit gains influence over *policy,* an outsider can also make the state subser-

---

203. [Literally, "the realm unto which it stretches itself sense-wise."]

204. [The word "spirit" is not intended religiously here.]

205. [Literally, "composed of pseudo-state-like acts."]

vient to his purposes—and that outsider can be God or the satan with equal ease.[206]

Sometimes you hear it said that a special vocation in the history of humanity is assigned to the state by divine governance of the world. That is not ruled out by the idea of state. The only thing you may not do is to construe it so that this vocation would be inserted *into the idea* of state by God. It is merely possible that the state, as it is according to its idea, is found by God to be suitable for serving him in the implementation of his purposes. And that is the reason why he can let states arise in the world and work in the direction of his intent.[207] That they will be subservient to him can be arrived at in two ways. [1] The world could be put together in such a way that whenever the state proceeds according to its own proper sense, it also advances the purposes of God, meaning that the state *must* advance the purposes of God in order to be able to maintain itself. (If we assume that moral education is the "divine vocation" of the state, then it could be arranged so that human beings have to be morally educated in order to fit in to the state.) [2] Another possibility would be that the representatives of the state used their position of power to enforce God's commandments in their sovereign territory. Then it would not be the state itself that stood in service to the divine purpose, but merely the fact that the state is there and you can borrow its authority in order to be able to realize purposes apart from those proper to the state.[208]

---

206. [The German makes it clear that "the satan" is not a proper name here. The wording follows the Hebrew usage in the opening chapters of the Book of Job.]

207. [When Stein says "can," she means that two ideas are compatible and can be affirmed simultaneously: (1) the idea of a God who influences the state, and (2) the idea of a state that already is what it is prior to divine intervention, yet has features through which God could subsequently influence it. This is an exercise in categorical logic. Stein does not mean to lay down conditions for what God himself can or cannot do. See below, Part II §6, for further discussion of God's governance of the world.]

208. [Literally, "to realize extra-stately purposes."]

Does the state have any such vocation, and if so, in *which* of the two possible ways is it fulfilled? This question is a purely factual one, which cannot be answered by a theory of the principles of the state. The theory can establish only that nothing of the kind is prescribed by the idea of the state, but neither is it ruled out. For this reason we must decline to found the theory of the state upon the "idea of the moral realm," in the way that F. J. Stahl designates as necessary in the "standard work" of conservative politics.[209] This idea can only be brought to the state from outside. There may be good grounds to do this. So the consequences that are drawn from this in practice can be completely justified. The only mistake is to think that they can be deduced from the idea of the state.

§3. The concrete pattern of the state as conditioned by factors other than the fabric of the state

a) Models of the state, in principle and empirically

The last remarks can serve to bring out the distinctiveness of our manner of examination in contrast to an *empirical* doctrine of the state. Jellinek, for example, distinguishes two possible directions of investigation. [There's] the *social* or historical-political, which is devoted to the establishment of objective and subjective (meaning "external" and "internal") events which comprise the life of the state. And [there's] a *juridical*, whose target is the "legal norms proceeding from the state and determined to control its institutions . . . , and the relationship of the real civil process to those legal norms of judgment."[210] Neither of the manners of examination envisioned here covers the problem as we have posed it. We're not interested in the actual facts of

---

209. See Friedrich Julius Stahl, *Die Staatslehre und die Principien des Staatsrechts,* third edition. (Heidelberg: Mohr, 1856). [The words "standard work" were written in English.]

210. See Jellinek, *Allgemeine Staatslehre,* p. 138. [See note 34 above, and Part I §1.b.]

state life (including the issuing of regulations of positive law, the contents of which are the concern of juridical research). Nor are we interested in the norms actually obtaining, to which those factual [arrangements] are supposed to conform.

We're trying instead to establish which of the factors identifiable in the actual composition of the subsisting state constitutes the state as such, and in this way to clarify that concept of the state which is presupposed by the empirical science of the state but not examined. This difference in the posing of the problem means that in no way are all the issues that are of importance for the empirical examination also to be examined by us. With empirical studies, for every kind of social group it must be investigated what sort of influence the group exerts upon the state and what sort of influence it undergoes from the state. With our studies, it suffices to define in principle the sphere of influence of the state and, on the other side, the amount of susceptibility to influence by individuals and groups possible in principle [for the state].[211]

In turn, that which is self-evident for empirical studies, and needs no investigation there, becomes a problem for us. Jellinek begins an investigation with a *definition* and all the rest ties into it. "A state is a multiplicity of human beings settled upon a delineated portion of the surface of the earth, provided with a ruling authority, and brought together into a unity by it."[212] And later, where reformulations and enlargements of the initial definition are dealt with, this happens on the basis of an empirical examination of subsisting states. In an examination on principles, the definition of a concept which is undergoing discussion can

---

211. [Stein reminds the reader that her intention is phenomenological. She is not describing particular states as they actually exist, so she does not have to cover every political system that has ever existed. She can be selective in her use of historical examples.]

212. See Jellinek, *Allgemeine Staatslehre,* p. 71. [See note 34, above.]

never initiate the investigation, but can only conclude it as its result; and facts have no role to play in the investigation itself. So for us, everything contained in that definition is questionable and in need of checking. The sense of every single term used in it calls for clarification.

We've already discussed the significance of the "ruling authority" for the composition of the state, and in fact we recognized it as constitutive. Conversely, it became clear through our analysis on principle that it won't do to designate the state as a "multiplicity of human beings." The state *encompasses* a range of persons (who need not necessarily be *human beings*), but those persons *are* not the state. On the other hand, it's not necessary that they are "brought together into a unity" for the first time by the state. A state can spring up on the basis of a union already obtaining. Which of the two is the case and, moreover, what kind of union it takes to serve as the basis for a state, are issues left open by the fabric of the state.

But this is still not to say that the one "possible" foundation is just as conducive to the existence of a concrete state pattern as the other is. It could very well be that in reality a state would be "viable" only under conditions that are not designated as necessary by its fabric [alone]. So in that case we would lay the responsibility on other factors involved in the composition of the concrete political system. The first [of those factors is] the fabric of the persons who belong to it. Thus *prior to* the empirical theory of the state[213] there are a whole series of problems that can be gotten at only from this perspective. These problems are just as important for the establishment of practical policy as they are for [theoretical political science].

---

213. [Political science as taught in most American universities today would fall into the category of "empirical theory of the state," as Stein describes it. She intends to examine the axioms and assumptions that are taken for granted in political science as we know it.]

b) Association and community as bases of the state

Here above all is the place to take up again the question treated earlier, whether the state is to be regarded as a pattern of community or as a pattern of association.[214] Associations are social federations that are founded voluntarily. Free persons enter into them by virtue of an act of willing, and they may withdraw from them again in the same manner. According to the rationalistic view, the state conforms to that type. Within it there prevails —for all individuals, in the ideal case, but at least for a portion of them—a rather precise overview of the composition and purpose of the whole and of their own position within it. And everything that they themselves would set about doing, or that was undertaken by the whole, every fluctuation within and every action without, would be the result of a deliberation and a free decision.

Such a formation would be conceivable. But it would not amount to a state, because the state is not called into existence through an act of willing by individuals—as an association is. Furthermore, such a formation would be continually at the mercy of the caprice of individuals and its existence would be threatened at every moment.[215] An example of this are those artificial "states" that are tailor-made by diplomats in their congresses and then are held together by the influence of outside coercion, but fall apart as soon as that pressure slackens. They also are states to the extent that the civil authority itself constitutes itself—even if on the basis of motives that were suggested to their possessors from outside —and to the extent that their claim to control is recognized. This is precisely why associational action is only a preparation for the founding of a state and does not coincide with the latter. In this

214. [The contrasting realities of community *(Gemeinschaft)* and association *(Gesellschaft)* were discussed in Stein's earlier treatise "Individual and Community," CWES 7:129-314.]

215. See Schleiermacher, *Staatslehre,* p. 179: ". . . Anarchy is founded by a contract which founds, simultaneously with the unification, the inclination of individuals to alter or topple what obtains." [See note 14 above, Part 1 §1.a.]

case it's the pre-state groundwork, and not the state itself, that would be associational. The acts of law-making are productive here. They *create* relationships that have no substance on their own.

When a state develops out of a community, on the contrary, the legal regulations are merely sanctions of relationships arising on their own. This state rests in a gravity of its own which is the foundation upon which the law-making will establishes itself as well as the source of the might that supports the state. Here the state comprises a community more or less extensively rationalized or (to say the same thing another way) reinforced with associational elements.

It still should be asked whether a state would also be conceivable in the mode of a community whose composition is not yet raised into the light of reasoning consciousness and is not made into the content of legal regulations. It looks as though sovereignty and therefore statehood must be omitted [if you eliminate] the law-giving will. Yet something of them is still there, to the extent that the pattern can be shaped not by an external force but from within, even if not by autonomous acts. With that, you have the material basis for a state, and at any time the breakthrough to freedom can occur, in our specific sense of the word.

c) The emergence of the state

The concrete commonwealth of the state is a self-developing pattern, just as a solitary person is. Therefore the investigation of the possible courses of development of that pattern goes along with the investigation of its ontic fabric. Let's not lose sight of the fact that the character of state as such, while undergoing no development itself, stands out more or less cleanly and completely in the concrete pattern of the state. If states were purely a product of legally effective acts, as contract theory holds, then it would be easy to settle the issue of their emergence and subsequent development. They would be called into existence by virtue of an optional act at a determinate point in time—in each case it would depend only on an accident of tradition whether it would be known to us or not. Likewise, any change in its fabric would be the result of an optional act determined purposefully at some point in time.

The question is more difficult if, as we hold, a state is no mere product of a law-making act (even though the legal constitution first makes it into a state in the full sense), but rather is linked to a preceding development of community. That development consists largely in the elaboration of social institutions. These are those peculiar, invisible, temporally determined objectivities of which we initially said that they owe their existence to persons but exist detached from persons. We have seen that they can be a product of positing acts. But is there yet another possibility for their emergence?

We know of objectivities that correspond to the legal and civil institutions in that they come to givenness[216] in the behavior of persons as usages in which their lives play themselves out, and in that they exist for a certain duration and then vanish again. We call them customs or practices, common law, and the like. In distinction to the institutions created through optional acts, with these you cannot state the point in time of their emergence or discontinuance. And this is so in principle, not just accidentally. They "come up" and "go away," and that coming and going is not the correlate of any act posited at a point in time.

Jellinek, writing in opposition to the view which "asserts the natural creation of law and state," says this view overlooks "the fundamental fact that no institution can emerge without a human will conscious of an aim and a purpose."[217] You can't take a position on that without clarifying, on the one hand, what is to be understood by "natural creation," and on the other, what is signified by the concern for a "will conscious of a purpose."

---

216. [To "come to givenness" is a technical phrase for the phenomenologists. It means that something has appeared: something is available to be known. The German idiom *es gibt,* usually translated "there is," literally means "it gives." What has "come to givenness" is there for the knowing.]

217. See Jellinek, *Allgemeine Staatslehre,* p. 47. [Stein inserted the words "an aim and" (*zeil- und*), which do not appear in Jellinek.]

Anyway, under "natural creation" you don't have to think of a "natural event" (in the strict sense, in which it stands in opposition to *mental* event). Suppose that in a circle of companions, a habit develops that in common undertakings one of them—and it's always the same one—takes over leadership and the others go along with his arrangements. If such a fixed order and division emerges, that is no "natural process." It is a mental process, in which certain direction-giving motives play a role: the greater activeness, the ability for initiative of the leader that impels him to action, determines the others in that it inspires their approval to follow him. Besides, the *sentient* lawfulness in the discrete participating individuals that we call "force of habit" plays a role:[218] the building up of dispositions toward manners of behavior that were first assumed under the guidance of original motivation, and of schemata laid down by the sentient occurrence. When these dispositions have become "fixed"—which requires some unspecified duration—then you can talk about a "custom" corresponding to them. The individuals are living according to this custom and it confronts them as a reality absolutely separate from themselves.

Now how does this mental-sentient process relate to the optionally chosen act through which a legal institution corresponding to the custom can be created? It is certainly correct not to rule out the will of individuals who in their living together develop certain usages. They pursue certain purposes with their

---

218. [*Psychische Gesetzlichkeit*, "sentient lawfulness," was discussed by Stein in her earlier treatise "Sentient Causality," CWES 7: 2-128. This term refers to the regular and predictable ways in which an individual living organism will feel and respond to physical processes occurring within the living body. Sentience is also open to the sentience of other organisms; but again, only in very specific ways. Stein argued that sentience exhibits a regularity or predictability that enables it to be studied scientifically. The force of habit is mentioned here as an example of a factor that operates within an individual organism and influences behavior, yet cannot be accounted for either in purely physical terms or in purely mental terms, according to Stein's view.]

behaviors, and it is possible that in this they are acting "voluntarily" in the specific sense, which means out of a freely made plan. The decisive thing is that in every case, what the purpose-setting will is aiming at *during* the development of a custom is not the development of a custom. While the legislative or law-making will has its eye on the mode of behaving that forms the content of the legal regulation, the focus is on something else entirely with the behavior that develops into a custom. The mode of behaving is entirely outside the frame. The possibility always obtains that the mental glance turns to the behavior, that the will imparts its sanction to the developed custom and renders it legally valid or even turns against it and stops it.

Thus if you understand the "natural" emergence not in opposition to what is mental, but rather as a non-"artificial" emergence, that is, as arising from deliberate positings, then it exhibits the typical developmental course of a community. According to our analysis, a commonwealth receives the character of state through the possession of sovereignty, which means the freedom to create its institutions by and for itself and to perform all its actions on its own. We speak of it even when the sovereign power is not expressly constituted as such and, on the other side, is not expressly recognized. It must merely exercise control and be unhindered in doing so. Furthermore, this includes the possibility in principle of fulfilling the constitution expressly at that point in time when it wishes to do so, and of its recognition.

d) The limits in principle to the state's might and the material conditions of its emergence

We were considering sovereignty to include the unrestricted power[219] to make law in an area of control circumscribed by reason of a proper constitution. And we were taking the possible

---

219. [*Macht,* "power," also means "might." This word is different from the words that Stein used in her earlier discussions of life power *(Kraft, Lebenskraft)* in CWES 4. *Macht* is power over life, but not the power of life itself. This distinction of terms is difficult to preserve in English but may be inferred from the context.]

content of legal regulations to include the establishment of particular modes of living and of living together in the community that represents the operative range of that power. We've said nothing about what areas of life the legal regulations can cover. However, the unrestrictedness of sovereignty implies that in principle there can be no limits to it (at least insofar as it's a question of limitation by another autonomous power), even if it can still be shown that in fact quite a lot may remain unaffected by the state's rulings and that too broad an expansion of the omnipotence of the state can be harmful to the state itself.

We have already touched upon those relationships as we were speaking of the linkages of the state to other social formations and specifically to the groups integrated into it and subordinated to it. The state encompasses communities and associations, groups of individuals of all possible kinds, which partly are contained in its region of power and partly encroach upon the region of power of another state, being partitioned by state borders in that case. For the most part, these groups emerge and are developed without any help from the state, and it's possible for them never to come into contact with the state during their entire duration, as is the rule for example with relationships among friends.

On the other hand, it could be that the state at some time lays its hand upon them. This is what happens with the family and marriage, through the development of civil marriage laws and through the state's rulings on the legal connections between parents and children. Even the law, which stands in such a close connection to the state, is not its domain alone. A private co-operative (a guild, for example), behaving as a will-endowed subject, can legislatively activate itself primarily to regulate its own organization as it sees fit. Private groups can even take charge of maintaining that which is recognized as law (not merely posited arbitrarily), the punishment of offenses, and the like, and indeed can represent the law-abiding group in a region beyond their own, or for the entire territory of a state. (Think of the secret

Vehme.[220]) The state within whose sovereign territory that happens remains unaffected as such, as long as the territory is not penetrated with overwhelming force against the will of the state, but [the intervention] is instead authorized by the state with the express or tacit proviso that the state can at any time suspend the law made by the other autonomous power and issue its own regulations. That is, as long as it's a matter of a self-limitation of the civil authority that does not signify any limitation of sovereignty.[221]

---

220. [The Vehmic tribunals, or *Vehmgerichte*, were medieval courts operating independently of local feudal lords. They became secret before gradually disappearing by the sixteenth century, but returned as a literary theme in nineteenth-century Romanticism. The idea of secretly sanctioned executions appealed to some disaffected elements in the troubled era between the wars in Germany. In Stein's day the secret Vehme was roughly the cultural equivalent of the Ku Klux Klan, but she may be using this term here only in its antique romantic sense. The so-called Parchimer Vehme (or Feme) Murder case made news in 1923. A young Nazi by the name of Rudolf Höss (whose Catholic parents had hoped he would become a priest) was convicted in this slaying and was sentenced to ten years in prison. Höss would go on to become commandant of the death camp at Auschwitz, where Stein would die in 1942. Höss himself was hanged at Auschwitz in 1947 for his crimes.]

221. It is a mistaken view of the relationship between state and law when Schleiermacher holds that the civil jurisdiction must give the citizens only the possibility of challenging the judgment of the state, and furthermore that two men [in a dispute] must be "at liberty to turn to someone whom both recognize as a referee to pronounce on the law for them without help from the state." See *Staatslehre,* p. 149. The granting of this liberty is placed entirely at the discretion of the state. To make a "must" out of it would signify a breach of sovereignty. [Although Stein cites p. 149, the passage appears on p. 144 of the edition Stein was using, and on p. 165 of the 1988 edition. See note 14 above in Part I § 1.a.]

That's how it is with everything that is created optionally or just susceptible to optional influences. It's only where the domain of voluntary arrangements comes to an end that limits in principle are set for the power of the state and [the scope of] its reach. The practical behavior of individuals can be restricted in a number of different ways by prescriptions of the state, and the form of their behavior can be sculpted. And in this way it is possible to direct the development of their personality along certain lines and to breed an artificial type of human being. Yet the personal distinctiveness that undergirds all personality development and sets strict limits to its possible variations will admit of neither prescribing nor proscribing. It unfolds itself in ever new differentiation: under the uniform type of the Prussian bureaucrat no less than in the Renaissance man growing up unfettered and asserting himself —breaking through the type, steadily diversifying anew from person to person, or, at worst, dormant within the type.

And just as it is with the personal distinctiveness, so it is with everything that is anchored in it, with everything that belongs to the realm of the soul: the person's attitudes, inner linkages between persons, and creations of the mind.[222] The state can

---

222. [*Geist*, "mind," can also mean "spirit." Stein now offers a working definition of what is included by the term "soul" *(Seele)*, specifying what she assigns to this realm. Earlier, in her 1916 dissertation on empathy (CWES 3:39-40), Stein had described the soul as a substantial unity. She wrote: "In our experiences, there is given to us something that is the basis for them, something that announces itself and its enduring properties in them. It is given as their identical 'carrier': that is the substantial soul." *([I]n unseren Erlebnissen ... gibt sich uns ein ihnen zugrunde Liegendes, das sich und seine beharrlichen Eigenschaften in ihnen bekundet, als ihr identischer "Träger": das ist die substanzielle Seele.)* Stein moved beyond this conception of the soul in her 1919 treatise on psychology (CWES 7:226-38), where the soul took on the function of mediating life-energy between the personal core and embodied sentience. Unlike the merely animal psyche, the soul is sensitive to values, with each soul receiving and cherishing values in its own unique way. This notion remains operative in the present text. Subsequently, in

forbid the persons standing under it to bind themselves to one another visibly under freely chosen usages. But the fact that they feel attracted to one another and that an inner community arises among them is something that no prohibition can impede, just as on the other hand, no commandment has the power to establish a community. Thus, finally, the state can also prescribe or proscribe forms of worship and public confession of this or that religion. But upon the relationship of the soul to God, no commandment or prohibition can exert any influence.[223]

Indeed, these relational networks are what Jellinek has in mind when he opposes the theory of the state's omnipotence. "Jurisprudence asserts that the sovereign state would be above every other organized authority and subject to none. But the ruler himself is subject to the mighty powers of social life, which do

---

her post-baptismal treatise *Potency and Act,* Stein would attempt to reconcile this functional notion with the scholastic doctrine of the soul as both form of the body and form of mental life. Yet she would maintain that the soul selectively opens itself to certain values and influences while closing itself to others (ESW 18:260-67; a forthcoming volume of CWES). Finally, in her maturework Stein would adopt St. Teresa's metaphor of the interior castle. The realm of the soul has—or is—a portal to divine life and value (ESW 6:39-68). In the present text, Stein already assigns interpersonal connections to the realm of the soul *(Reich der Seele),* thus placing them off-limits to the state. The notion of soul is further developed below; see the excursus on guilt following Part II §4.a.; see also Part II §6.]

223. [This is meant as a purely descriptive statement, in which the phenomenologist points to a common human experience. The statement is not prescribing or demanding anything. Stein does *not* say that the state *should not* interfere with the inner connections: she points out that such interference is impossible in principle. God is mentioned as the ultimate case of personal relation, but on a continuum that includes other inner personal ties as well. The imperviousness of the soul to state interference is depicted as a structural feature the human capacity for interpersonal relationship as such. Once again, the religious case is not a special case but is confirmed by other examples of interpersonal relationships.]

not operate in the mode of a consciously autonomous power."[224]

What's missing here—as everywhere in Jellinek—is the distinction between the limits *in principle* of the state's sphere of influence, and the *factual* relations of dependence in which the state and the other social groups and the individuals are standing. Suppose that *in fact* none of the empirically known states were providing for the musical training of their citizens. That is not to say that there *could be* no state that would create the appropriate institutions [for musical training] and declare their use to be obligatory. However, it would be absurd if that state wanted to prescribe for all individuals alike that they had to come into the world with a certain musical talent. On the other hand, suppose there were historical proof that the extant states are completely conditioned by certain social groups that comprise them or of whom they share a part. That still would not show that those relationships of dependence *must* obtain and that in principle it would be inconceivable for a state to owe its entire structure to its own regulations.[225]

The self-limitations of civil authority of which we've already occasionally spoken require a special investigation. They fall under the area of liberty itself. They are coherent with the peculiarly backwards obligation that pertains to all law-making and with the anchoring of that obligation in an addressee. With each of its regulations the state commits itself to keep those regulations, and also allows a claim to arise in the persons in its sovereign sphere for this to happen. All who belong to the state have a share in that common and so-called formal claim for the observance of civil law. Besides that, there are content-specific claims of individual persons or groups or even of the whole civil community according to the content of the legal regulations and their addressees.

---

224. See Jellinek, *Allgemeine Staatslehre,* p. 125.

225. [Although Stein has strongly supported community, and even an ethnic community, as a viable basis for a state, she insists here that social homogeneity is by no means essential to a state.]

These include the claims that are founded through the establishment of state agencies and the rights[226] that correspond to them. If a state is constituted as a hereditary monarchy, then that gives rise to a claim for whoever is heir to the crown at the time to be recognized as the representative of the state, and to the right for acts to be performed in his name—either alone or in common with other assigned agencies. Any constitution represents such a self-commitment of the state, through which a whole series of "laws for setting up agencies" are founded (to use Bernatzik's term). Thereby the state marks off, out of the range of possibilities that are available to it for the performance of its acts, those certain ones to which it commits. But it has to be maintained here that this committing alone is the real business of the state,[227] and that the subjective rights arising from it owe their origin to the law of the state.

Bernatzik disregards that fact when he says of the communes[228] in some states: "On one hand, they have proper laws

---

226. [*Rechte,* "rights," could also mean "laws." The translation depends upon the context. In the example to follow, the monarch would be the state's agent or agency *(Organ).*]

227. [*Sache des Staates,* "real business of the state," is a phrase that flags the heart of the argument for Stein's phenomenological readers. The motto of the Phenomenological Movement was "to the things themselves!" *(zu den Sachen selbst).* In effect, Stein asserts that the focus of a phenomenological inquiry into the state must be centered upon the state's self-establishing choice of the sort of state that it will be.]

228. [*Kommunen,* "communes," are local administrative districts in some parts of Europe. In the context of the 1890 article cited here, the term may also allude to the Paris Commune of 1871. This anarchist resistance movement lasted only a few weeks, but it was much analyzed by political theorists such as Karl Marx, Mikhail Bakunin, and Friedrich Engels, who hailed it as the first dictatorship of the proletariat or working class. Poor people in Paris took up arms against invading Prussians and attempted to enact social reforms. By

without setting up agencies. On the other hand, they are *agencies* of the state that nevertheless . . . have for their competency a proper *law*, and finally they are agencies of the state *without* proper laws for the relevant competency."[229] For one thing, what you've got here with the laws of the communes are merely differences in content and not differences in their legal character. All subjective rights (insofar as they can make a claim to validity in a positive-law sense) are ultimately anchored in the state.[230] There may be communions that are older than the state to which they belong, and they may have retained from their past the exercise of

---

most accounts, their failure was owing to a lack of effective organization, including the disciplined use of military force. The Paris Commune opposed the bourgeois institutions of both the state and the church, and several prominent priests were brutally executed. Then the Commune itself was violently overthrown, and the death toll is put at 30,000. The Paris Commune was the model, or at least an inspiration, for soviets of workers and soldiers organized after the Russian Revolution in 1917. Stein has little to say about socialism as such in this treatise. This perhaps has less to do with her favorable view of Prussian monarchy than with the fact that a socialist friend and former student was preparing a treatise that might touch upon the subject. See Gerda Walter, "Zur Ontologie der sozialen Gemeinschaften (mit einem Anhang zur Phänomenologie der sozialen Gemeinschaften)," *Jahrbuch für Philosophie und phänomenologische Forschung* 6 (1923) 1-158.]

229. See Bernatzik, "Kritische Studien," p. 305. [See above, note 154. The word for "law" *(Recht)* can also be translated "right" in every case. Stein capitalizes upon this ambiguity in Bernatzik's argument. While Bernatzik seems to be talking about the law, Stein proceeds to interpret this quote as if it were about rights.]

230. ["Subjective rights" for Stein are those which accrue to an individual subject by virtue of a social act, such as a promise. She is not saying that the state is the source of rights. She is saying merely that the ability to make an effective claim based upon rights is an ability that is anchored in the state. Any such claim gets its real traction from the positive law of the state.]

certain functions.[231] The exercise of those functions is *legal* only to the extent that it is *permitted* to the communions by the state (which can occur even tacitly). And in the absence of a [state] agency, a right is *legal* only for as long as the state abstains from taking over the function in question and maybe lets the function be exercised by the communions in the name of the state instead of licensing them for the exercise [of this function] on their own.[232] There is no such thing as a state agency without a proper right to the pertinent competence.[233] There's a difference between [two sorts of] rights to set up agencies. [Agencies may be set up through rights] that a communion has claimed on its own. [Or they may be set up through rights] that were transferred to the communion by the state without being sought (thinking perhaps of the withdrawal of state sponsorship) and that the communion probably never would make operative on its own. That does not

---

231. [This may be an oblique reference to the church's traditional position of prestige and privilege in the bourgeois state, which was criticized by the Paris Commune of 1871. *Gemeinde,* "communion," can also mean "parish," "congregation," or even "commune." Above, the topic was introduced with the specific German political term *Kommune.* The more general term *Gemeinde* now extends the discussion to all quasi-governmental initiatives that arise among the people apart from the state itself.]

232. [The grammatical structure of this sentence is unclear. Stein seems to have in mind a function such as education. Churches conducted schools before the rise of modern states, but continue to do so today in the name of the state (in some countries) or through licensing by the state (in other countries). "Public" schools in the United States are supported by local taxes and administered by local school boards, with input from private groups such as parents' associations and teachers' unions, unless and until the state or federal government steps in to overrule their policies. In these instances, the "private" groups exercise authority only to the extent permitted by the state.]

233. [In other words, if there's a state agency, it has to have the legal competence to do whatever it was designed to do.]

change the fact that in the very moment when it is entrusted with the exercise of a state function, the communion also is equipped with a right to its exercise.[234]

Alongside of the "backwards" commitment of the state through its own proper right, we've come up with something else within the sphere of liberty: being commissioned upon the recognition of those to whom the state's claim of control is addressed. Without that recognition, we said, the state could not exist. This has to be made more precise. You can talk about an "injury" to the state in two senses: in case of a "transgression" of its legislation and in case of dispositions and actions whose whole point is to oppose the state itself and *deny its authority* (which need not be the case at all with the mere transgression). A transgression all by itself does not annul sovereignty, any more than the freedom of a person is annulled by "letting herself drift" and not relying on her own initiative. Just as the person can at any time take "control of herself" again, so the inviolability of sovereignty is expressed in the *right to punish* when state regulations are broken.

But it's different when the civil authority's right to regulate is openly disputed or made out to be null through deliberate non-observance of legislation. In that case, the sovereignty is in dispute and the existence of the state is placed in question. If it has means at its disposal that are capable of wringing the withheld recognition from the recalcitrant elements, and if it makes use of them, the state gets through the condition of uncertainty and achieves a new stabilization. If such means are lacking, then the state is annulled even if the survival of certain state functions may obscure that fact.

The possibility of the annihilation of the state lets us consider the problem of "recognition" from yet another angle. So far we've been examining only the dependency of sovereignty upon the recognition of those who belong to the sovereign territory of the

---

234. [In Stein's view, the social act of entrusting the function has brought into being the subjective right to exercise that function on the part of the communion so entrusted.]

state. But since sovereignty was for us synonymous with the freedom of the state in its self-configuration, sovereignty also has a face turned "to the outside." Sovereignty determines the relationship of the state to other states. Doesn't the state depend upon their recognition, too? This must be investigated.

In actual exchanges among states, a newly founded state (or a new civil authority) isn't even deemed to be legitimate until it is recognized by the governments of other states. Yet it can't be conceded that subsisting states have a *right* to participate in the foundation of a new one. The state can subsist only by virtue of its own proper right, as was stressed again and again. But the demand to be recognized within the borders defined by its own authoritative decree is directed not only to the autonomous subjects belonging to its sovereign territory, but also to those standing outside, by whom the state likewise could be challenged. To define a sphere of control for itself means to withdraw that sphere from the possible aggression of other sovereign powers, and this is not possible without their consent. Suppose that the delineation of a sphere of control were given through defining a foreign one. This would be a limitation of sovereignty, if it did not come about as a self-delineation, and this happens in the mode of consent. This consent, just like that of the persons who belong to the sphere of control in question, need not be expressly performed. If the foreign governments engage in contact with the newly founded one, then the consent is implicit in that. And it even suffices if they tacitly leave to it the sphere of control that it claims for itself, without attempting an intervention or even just retaining the right to intervene.

On the other hand, suppose that an objection arises from some quarter against the establishment of a new civil authority—whether it be against the mode that the civil authority assumes, or against the manner of marking off of its territory. That puts the state *in suspenso*.[235] Its existence is not secured until the state finds ways and means to bring the others around to

---

235. [*In suspenso* is Latin for "in suspense." The legality of the state becomes uncertain.]

consent. For as long as that is not the case, for as long as others are interfering with government in its territory or reserve the right to do so, the commonwealth that wishes to constitute itself as a state may be functioning like a state in some respects, and all state functions could even be set up and ready to go—that changes nothing. Existence as a state has not yet fully prevailed.

e) State and political functions. Decline of the state

That leads us to a whole new issue. How is it possible for state or *political functions* to go on without the presence of a state?[236] We find commonwealths that exhibit such functions on the way to becoming a state and while declining from being a state. They make it comprehensible that the constitutive significance of sovereignty could be misunderstood, and that somebody might want to claim that a non-sovereign commonwealth was a state. This view is not decisively demolished until we can show that neither the concept of political function nor that non-sovereign commonwealth itself can be comprehended except by starting with the sovereign state.

It makes good sense for us to understand political functions as the achievements of the state or within the state that are indispensable for its existence, and the agencies of the state as the persons or corporate bodies needed by the state as carriers of those functions. The most important agency of the state is the

---

236. [One philosophical context for this question is the Marxist doctrine of the withering away of the state through inexorable historical processes. Even before Marx, however, the issue provoked discussion among German Idealist philosophers. J.G. Fichte, whose political views are discussed below in Part II, wrote that "life in the state is not one of man's absolute aims. The state is, instead, only a *means for establishing a perfect society*, a means which exists only under specific circumstances. Like all those human institutions which are mere means, the state aims at abolishing itself. *The goal of all government is to make government superfluous.*" See *Fichte: Early Philosophical Writings,* trans Daniel Breazeale (Ithaca: Cornell University Press, 1988), p.156. See also note 267, below.]

government, which means the civil authority through whose self-institution the state makes its appearance and through which it makes itself heard. The function of the civil authority is the management of the state, which includes arranging for state actions, law-making (= setting up norms for social life within its sphere of sovereignty), and seeing to it that the regulations and commands of the state are carried out.

Does it make any sense to speak of a government in a non-state commonwealth? No doubt there are actions of the whole here (for example, if a city concludes delivery contracts to cover the needs of its citizens, or devises welfare institutions, and the like). There can even be agencies that initiate such actions in the name of the whole. But the commonwealth does not collapse if it lacks a central agency (or any agency at all). Think of a village commune whose members do things as a community (cultivate their field, celebrate festivals, and the like). Thus the commune makes its appearance as a whole, and there is no agency that represents this whole and manages its activities. Its existence requires no operative norms to govern its life, and therefore also no source to issue such norms and no executive arm to provide for their enforcement. The sphere of state is completely missing here.

On the other hand, the sphere of state is always already in a certain manner intruding when there's a commonwealth that exhibits a fixed "autonomous organization." Autonomous management as such, the direction of community activities, in itself has a reference to an ultimate center that does not tie in to any further stage. There are communities where the ultimate center responsible for their activities is not within themselves: they are then carried by a state sphere that intrudes into them, but they themselves are not states. Or, they have their center of gravity within themselves and are not directed from outside, but a sovereign civil authority has yet to be constituted in them: then the breakthrough to the state sphere is not yet completed, although it already makes itself noticeable in the life and in the organization of the community. This shows up in the command authority as well as in legislation and adjudication. Since all operative law refers back to a law-making subject, wherever law is in effect and is enforced there must also be a subject that is authorized, either on its own or from elsewhere, to make and enforce law. In the one case, the sector where the law is in effect is a state, and in the other case it's a community standing in a relationship of dependence to a state.

The command authority is not to be detached from the law, inasmuch as command authority itself is an instance of a subjective right and consequently refers back to legally effective acts. Where there's a recognized command authority (and only there can you talk about political functions), that command authority subsists either by virtue of its own law—which means, laws made by the command authority itself—or by virtue of foreign law, and thus always in liaison with a sovereign civil authority.

Therefore the political functions are inseparably bound to the state, as we believe the state must be understood. If those functions are found as well in commonwealths that are not to be viewed as states in our sense of the word, how that is possible can be comprehended under various stipulations:

1. if the commonwealths are embedded in a state and the political functions that they exercise are anchored in the state;
2. if they are "on their way to state," which means pressing toward constitution as a state according to the proper sense of their own organization;
3. if they are the remainder left over after the disintegration of the state, as it were.

We've yet to consider that last case, and some words about it are still to be said. It's possible for one state to be conquered by another, which takes over the command authority in its place, but allows the disestablished commonwealth to operate again as broadly as before. A central authority with all kinds of political functions could be permitted to the disestablished commonwealth. It's only that the central authority now no longer subsists by virtue of the commonwealth's own law, but rather by virtue of a foreign law. Then a commitment of the political functions obtains in a twofold sense: to the destroyed state, which developed them, and to the ruling state, in which they are newly anchored.

Furthermore, there's a danger of a dissolution of a state from within: that the civil authority is no longer recognized, that its regulations are no longer obeyed. The active or passive resistance of the citizens need not extend to all functions of the state. It is conceivable that to a great extent they make broad use of available civil institutions like schools, libraries, insurance, and the like; that in their legal dealings they have recourse to the civil courts, and evade the state's authoritative decisions only where their private interests appear to be jeopardized. Where the punishment of such a continual denial of the authority of the state is no longer possible, in our view the state is to be considered dissolved. In that case the commonwealth still survives but you no longer have it bound to an *extant* state. However the functions still retained in power are *meaningful* only in the context of a complete state and according to their origin they refer back to such a state. Nevertheless, those connections between state and sovereignty, as they pressed themselves upon us, are not to be gained from an investigation of the factually available states.[237]

f) State and land

In his definition of the state, Jellinek named as a constitutive factor the "portion of the surface of the earth" to which the state is bound. We still have to investigate how that can be so. The issue is part of a set of problems having to do with the natural basis of the state. There are close connections between the quality of the countryside and the quality of the populace that still have to be discussed. It appears that the "nature" of the countryside influences that of the inhabitants, and furthermore, that it imposes certain requirements on the number and the character of the

---

237. [In other words, these are connections of meaning and so require phenomenological investigation. They are not connections of cause and effect, and so cannot be gotten at through observation of events occurring within or among real states. On the contrary, to understand such events, you first must understand what people have in mind. What people mean by "state" or "law" will determine what they are trying to do through their observable actions.]

people which must be fulfilled if the existence of a state in this region is to be possible.

Prior to that issue, however, there lies another one, whether then in general the dependence upon a land area is constitutive for the state as such. Discussion of this question is not made unnecessary, of course, by the fact that the modern states, which we naturally tend to think of first, possess a fixed territory and exhibit the influence of that territory in their entire fabric. Investigation shows that the question is to be answered negatively. For one thing, note that you can't dismiss the possibility of a state whose foundation would be purely mental persons. We could imagine a well organized realm of minds whose firmly arranged modes of life arise from its own authority. We could rediscover all possible modes of state here. As long as their operations do not extend in space—which is not excluded in principle—they are free from any dependence upon space at all and therefore from dependence upon any part of space.[238] And even if they involve themselves in a certain manner with space, for example to influence the sequence of events on a planet, they still need not bind themselves to that spatial body, because they retain their unassailable and invisible zone of sovereignty from which their operations extend into the visible world, just as an earthly state can extend its operations to sectors that do not belong to its sphere of sovereignty (perhaps in the mode of commerce).

Things are different when the persons who form the foundation of a state possess a bodily configuration of some kind. Bodily

---

238. [*Raum,* "space," does not mean outer space. It means the physical world. Philosophically, matter is defined as that which extends in space, having some size. Mind, on the contrary, does not take up space and has no dimensions that could be physically measured. Stein invites the reader to imagine a state composed entirely of citizens who had minds but no bodies, and therefore need have no dealings with the physical world. This is a thought experiment designed to show that since such a state can be conceived without logical contradiction, the requirement of having land cannot be part of the essence of the state.]

configured individuals are always necessarily in a spatial sphere, and indeed in the kind of spatial sphere that is commensurate with their configuration. And if they form a state, then that state must have such a spatial sphere as its sovereign territory, because otherwise it would not be in a position to secure for itself the free disposition of the modes of life of its citizens. And it would always run a risk of falling into dependence upon a foreign autonomous power, which means of losing its sovereignty and therefore its character as state.

Based on that—to come back again to talking about earthly relations—we can consider the question of whether highly organized nomadic hordes can be recognized as states. Certainly it is not necessary for the state that the same territory always forms its sovereign territory. The state requires only enough maneuvering room for its citizens. But in principle that could be a shifting portion of the surface of the earth. A couple of things are to be noted in that regard:

1. Enough space must be available that is not yet claimed by other powers. As soon as a nomadic tribe is directed to settle itself in the territory of another state, it falls into dependence upon that state and thereby is deprived of the possibility in principle of forming a state of its own (unless it succeeds in displacing the state that's there and setting up one of its own in its place).

2. If a people organized as a state has wedded itself to a territory, then the concrete pattern of the state carries the stamp of the land. If the land is now abandoned by the people and they settle in another area, then the character of the concrete pattern can change so much that you can't speak of the same state but must say: the old state went under and a new one arose. However, the fact that a specific state pattern cannot outlive the giving up of its territory does not prove that being bound to a specific territory belongs to the state as such.

This clarifies the main question of the relationship between state and land. Now we have to investigate the modes of dependence of the two that are possible in principle. Just as the boundedness of the state to any territory at all is the consequence of the bodily figuration of the individuals belonging to it, so also are all other possible linkages between the two to be understood only on that basis. The state needs the land inasmuch as the citizens need it. And the demands that are to be placed upon the quality of the land at any given time depend upon what particular kind of needs they are. Let's imagine persons with phantom bodies, which means purely visually qualified without material composition. Then what they must demand for their spatial sphere of sovereignty would be only the area, lighting, and so forth that would be sufficient for guaranteeing them the possibility of an unhindered unfolding of their visual appearance.

On the other hand, if we take persons of the human type, with a material body that is directed to replenish its composition from the material world in which it is placed, then a certain material quality is required in the sovereign territory of the state. It must contain the materials that the individuals require in a sufficient quantity, or materials that can be converted into those necessary. This is where the *place of the economy* in the structure of the state becomes clear. According to its original sense, economy is the organization of the satisfaction of needs. At the same time this shows the reciprocal dependence of land and inhabitants. If the "raw materials" of an area do not suffice for the satisfaction of the needs, then there are various ways of providing for their satisfaction.

1. Means can be found to convert the materials available in the land into those needed.
2. New land can be acquired that supplies sufficient material.[239]
3. The material needed can be obtained from other lands. The third path runs the risk of falling into dependence and ceasing to be a self-sufficient political system, unless it's a case where the exchange is also needed on the other side.

---

239. [This is the path of colonization or annexation. Stein defers the question of whether the targeted land already has inhabitants who are using its materials for their own support. Nor does she mention the path of limiting the growth of the population to a level that the land can support.]

That *one* of those paths must be walked is a constraint that the quality of the land exerts upon all those who inhabit it.[240] To express it with precision: The quality of the land is the motivational basis for the direction taken by the activity of all those who inhabit it. Which of the various possible paths is chosen no longer depends upon the nature of the land (or at any rate not in the same mode), but rather upon the particular disposition of human beings. Physical power will press toward the path of conquest; intelligence and industry, toward the path of possibly a rational evaluation of the products of the land; a certain mental agility and flexibility, toward the path of commerce.

Certain properties of the land not yet considered (such as location on the sea or, conversely, isolation by other [features of the] landscape) can be added as motives for the decision in the one or the other direction, and can support the development of one or the other type lying within the range of developmental possibilities.[241] When the natural foundations are completely identical, what makes the difference is personal disposition. Whether that [disposition] itself still depends on the nature of the land is a further question.[242] In any case, this dependence would no longer have the form of motivation; only a causal connection would come under consideration.

It would be conceivable for an influence upon the sentient predispositions of a human being to issue from the material quality of the body—which for its part is composed out of the

---

240. [*Bewohnerschaft,* "all those who inhabit it," suggests that this constraint is felt by the populace at large, not singly by individual inhabitants (*die Bewohner*).]

241. [For example, a country with poor soil but lots of harbors, like Greece, would foster the development of a flexible *type of person* with an agile mind. Persons of that type would tend to choose to engage in commerce by sea. The mechanism by which this happens is only partly causal. Physical causality works together with a contrasting process: motivation.]

242. [This question has to do with the individual person. Above, Stein was talking about a *type* of person.]

stuff of the material environment in which it grew up. Then in a certain sense the character would be a "product of nature." Whether that is so for the character would be decided only after comprehensive investigations of the psycho-physical connections, which we cannot pursue here.[243] Besides that, there's the possibility of a *mental* influence of nature upon the person who grows up in it: owing to an impact upon the temperament from the "character" of the countryside, its gloominess or gracefulness, and the like. Imagine a landscape that, according to its physical quality, would be suitable to stimulate the inhabitants to highest activeness, since strenuous activity was required to wring the necessary produce from it. [Conceivably, it might have the opposite effect. Maybe it] affects them by its character in a paralyzing way and does not allow them to achieve sufficient organization, while an enterprising conqueror puts them to work with no further ado.

The transformation of the soil (through irrigation, planting, and the like), along with all other human institutions that have as their purpose to make the available material productive for the satisfaction of needs, submit the land to the influence of the inhabitants so that it can undergo a profound change and cease to be pure "nature." (Thus the science whose object is the lands of the earth—geography—is not a natural science, according to its full substance. It takes the "earth" as it finds it, as an arena of historical events and with all the traces of the history that has transpired upon it.) Therefore the territory of a state cannot be adduced as a natural basis—any more than its population can—without further qualification. Rather, both land and populace are "mixed" objectivities in which nature and mind both have a share. Only through an abstractive examination is that which is

---

243. [Stein apparently laid the groundwork for such investigations in her earlier treatises. See CWES 7. The conspicuous lack of a reference to that work at this point is an indication that Stein intended to do further work on this issue, building upon the earlier treatises. See her later work *Potency and Act,* a forthcoming volume of CWES.]

nature within them to be extracted and be allowed treatment in a natural-science manner.[244]

The economy belongs to the areas that the state can organize on its own or leave to the activity of individuals and private groups, according to the circumstances. If the state presents itself as an economic subject,[245] it may correctly be said that the state itself fashions a territory for itself—within limits which the natural factors define. The face of the landscape is altered no less when various peoples and formations of states become detached from its soil, than the character of a people changes under the influence of different territories that it inhabits, one after the other. If the economy is left to private initiative, the state still retains the prerogative of regulatory interference. And if the state does not involve itself as a subject in economic life, it will still prescribe or forbid certain practices for the economy, in that it issues legal regulations.

There's one territory at any given time that belongs to the state "in a natural manner," even if the state is not yet its owner, legally or factually. It's to be understood from this "pre-established harmony" that the state will endeavor to bring it under its power. The circumference of this territory is first defined by the extent of the needs. If a territory does not yield what its inhabitants need, even when all possibilities of conversion and usage of the available materials are exploited, then an expansion is necessary so that the state does not let itself fall into subjection [to another state].

Besides that, one more principle of demarcation obtains:

---

244. [Nature as such, in isolation from cultural and psychological influences, cannot be found in our world. The natural sciences always practice a preliminary step of artificially subtracting cultural and psychological factors, so that "data" can be isolated for study. All scientific data are produced through such subtractive steps.]

245. [*Wirtschaftssubjekt*, "economic subject," means a decision-maker in economic matters. Such a state would participate actively in business and trade activities.]

"geographical individuality" (in Karl Ritter's sense[246]). The earth is divided into a series of continents and countries which present themselves in self-contained unities. If the borders of states intersect such a geographic individual, on both sides the demand will arise for the destroyed unity to be re-established or for the natural unity to be transformed into a legal one. It's debatable whether that geographic unit is synonymous with a closed "area of need" (which means an area united by the ability to cover the needs of its inhabitants in all respects). But deciding this issue is not of critical significance, and we don't wish to investigate it here.

Even if the geographic unit were a unity only according to its perceived tangible shape and without any reference to human needs, it would come into consideration as a contributing motive for the demarcation of the state's territory, and its bisection would constitute a moment of uneasiness and of danger for the states that were party to it. Here we have an analogy to the significance of the people as basis of the state. A state can just as well encompass several geographic units as several peoples, and they can be peacefully taken up in it.[247] On the other hand, the state can slice through the unity of a people just like that of the countryside. But that renunciation of its natural basis always creates an "irredenta"[248] and thereby a threat to its own existence.

---

246. [Stein may mean Carl Ritter. See his *Geographical Studies,* trans. William L. Gage (Cincinnati: Van Antwerp, Bragg and Co., 1861). The same translator also published an abridgement of Ritter's work, *The Comparative Geography of Palestine and the Sinaitic Peninsula* (New York: D. Appleton and Co., 1866).]

247. [*In ihm aufgehoben,* "taken up in it," could also mean "neutralized within it" or even "dissolved in it."]

248. [*Irredenta* is a loaded political term. When a state is composed of a majority ethnic group some of whose members live in another region separated from the state, a movement may arise to "liberate" the separated population by annexing the distant region to the state where the ethnic group in question is the majority. The region in dispute is called *irredenta* or "unredeemed" from the

The unity of the land and the unity of the people are not entirely unconnected to one another. We saw that the "character" of a land (in both senses) influences the character of its inhabitants. Under that influence there arises a personal type that we can designate as a "race." If the representatives of one racial type live in a community, and if this community is comprehensive enough to be active as a culturally creative personality, then we have a *people* that has arisen upon the soil of the land. Not *every* unity of the landscape need be the carrier of a people. There are geographic units of various sizes. The smaller ones do not offer space enough for so comprehensive a community as a people must have. The community that arises on their soil is merely a *"tribe."* The unity of a people is not produced until several tribes together produce it in that they blend with each other.

On the other hand, there are geographic units that—joined in a series of partial individuals—are so extended that several peoples emerge within them. Then there is one unity encompassing peoples which, inasmuch as it has to do with a unity of type, falls under the concept of race. If one intellectual community encompassing the closer communities develops out of that, then we can speak of a cultural sphere founded upon the unity of race. (The cultural sphere can in principle extend even beyond the limits of the racial unity thus broadly extended.)[249]

---

perspective of the state that wants to annex it. In Stein's day, Germanic and Slavic populations lived side by side in many regions of Europe. One example was the Sudetenland, a part of the present-day Czech Republic, which was claimed and annexed to Germany by Adolf Hitler in 1938.]

249. [Thus for Stein, a race is a type of human being. Race arises out of adaptation to the physical environment of a particular country. In turn, race gives rise to an intellectual or mental community that can extend beyond the country of origin of the race, and can even extend beyond the members of the race itself. The cultural sphere, then, is the medium for sharing among peoples of different races.]

g) Segmentation by status

When concrete patterns of states are considered, the thing about their composition that particularly catches your eye is their peculiar segmentation. As in an organism, their manifold parts work together for the life of a whole that is dependent upon their particular functionings. All "organic" theories of the state have taken this as their point of departure and considered it to be a cardinal point. Nevertheless we have seen that the configuration of the concrete political system is not determined through the character of *state* as such alone. And so with the organic segmentation as well we will have to examine the extent to which the configuration is on account of the character of *state,* and how much of it some other factor is to be considered responsible for.

The primary differentiation is prescribed by the framework of the state without any thing further: the differentiation into civil authority and citizens, into government and governed, where it is not excluded in principle that one person might unite both roles in herself. Yet as a rule they are imparted to different persons. The functions of the government are already sufficiently familiar to us. It is the central agency in which the will of the state is concentrated and from which that will radiates. The government has to manage the actions of the whole, give them a push and maybe a prescription for the manner of carrying them out. Moreover, the government is the ultimate wellspring of the entire law operative in the territory of the state. The function of the governed as such is only to recognize the government and to follow its commands. Where there are persons who harbor an impulse to refuse to obey,[250] the state needs new agencies for securing its existence.

---

250. [Literally, "where stimuli toward refusal of obedience are living in the persons." Here and in the next paragraphs, Stein argues for the necessity of armed forces: police as well as defensive military forces. But contrasting arguments appear below. See pp. 175-6, where Stein asserts that competing values cannot be resolved by an external struggle and the state has a duty to consider all the values affected by its actions. See also pp. 143-4, on the danger of using state power to

To assure compliance with its commands and regulations, a physically coercive authority becomes necessary, an armed force. There is also need—to put it Platonically[251]—of *guardians* who protect the law against transgressions on the part of the citizens as well as against violation by outside enemies.

Let's start by considering only the first possibility. The armed force of the state must be large enough to be capable of stopping any opposing autonomous operations. How large in number it must be depends on various circumstances: on the total number of the population whose seditious aspirations it is supposed to be suppressing; on the character of the people and especially their inclination to comply with state order or protest against it and to give in to physical coercion or fight back; and finally on the difference in character of the "guardians" and the rest of the people. For the last case it's important how the state assembles its armed forces: whether it makes the activity of guarding into a vocation proper, or whether it presses members of other vocations into service as guardians for a certain time. All of these circumstances are "imponderables." They can be vaguely estimated, but no one can determine them exactly. And even the vague estimates have the character of probability, not final certainty. Yet the existence of states depends upon the correct estimate of these circumstances. If the representatives of the state guess wrong about them, they expose the state to the danger of annihilation.

The difficulty increases if we now consider the necessity of protection against external enemies. The state may not allow its laws to be thwarted by those of a foreign power. That is the case

---

maintain the current political system. Instead of armed repression or ideological conflict, she recommends the alternative of reasoning about the material basis of the state.]

251. [This is a reference to Plato's well-known work the *Republic*. It depicts an ideal state where the guardians or ruling class have absolute authority but no property of their own and no families. The guardians include the "philosopher-kings" and the police. Plato was an older contemporary of Aristotle who wrote in the fourth century B.C.E.]

if those affiliated with a foreign state set foot in its territory and do not comply with its directives, but rather act according to those of their own civil authority. The state that does not wish to relinquish its existence must provide means to prevent that possibility. And the power that is required in order to repulse a foreign power is to be estimated analogously to that [amount of power] which has to guarantee the maintenance of the laws internally: according to the number and the character of the foreign peoples and their relationship, respectively, to those of the homeland.

The state requires an armed force for the maintenance of its laws and for the maintenance of its territory. As we saw, the two support each other as well as the maintenance of sovereignty. But there may be more to it than keeping the factual ownership intact and undiminished. The state must be strong enough to secure for itself as much land as is required for the preservation of its existence.

In the armed force we have an "agency" that is required for its own sake, on the basis of the quality of people and the other material conditions that the state has to reckon with. But that's not just true of the armed force alone. Further agencies are required for the maintenance and execution of the legal norms as well as implementation of decisions of the state. For one thing, there must be legal *experts* who preserve and transmit the knowledge of what the law is within the state. And *executive* agencies are needed as occasions arise to apply the law or to see to it that things are done according to the law.

The military and the "office holders" (in precisely the established sense) are "ranks" that represent the form of the state itself, the civil order. Besides those, others emerge which conceivably could have a life prior to the state or outside of it, and which present the material for a concrete state pattern. The community of individuals living in the state exhibits a segmentation following the principles of the division of labor. To explain the origin of the state, many writers (ever since Plato) refer to individuals' need for assistance. The necessity of creating an organization for satisfying needs individually, in which one undertakes this work and another undertakes that work for the collective, is supposed to have led to the foundation of the state. We can set aside what this quality of individuals might mean for the genesis of the state. Surely we would be able to let it count as a motive that speaks in favor of the recognition of a self-constituting civil authority by its presumptive subjects. That doesn't change the fact that the fabric of the state as such and the quality of persons are two factors that cannot be derived from any other factor. The persons could be equipped in such a way that the satisfaction of their needs is possible only in the framework of the state. (This might be because the "antisocial" impulses that stand in the way of any community regulation of their concerns are so strong that only an authority furnished with means of coercion is able to restrain them). That doesn't make the state an "invention" that human beings "thought up" as a *remedium*[252] for the shortcomings of their nature. The state would be suitable as a *remedium* only by virtue of that which it is in its own right.

In principle it's conceivable to have a labor-dividing community, a segmentation according to vocational ranks, even apart from the state. Insofar as it's a matter of "material" needs whose satisfaction is supposed to be made possible through the division of labor, only the provision for this satisfaction—the "economy" —is a possible community affair; the needs themselves are simply individual. On the other hand, in the area of mental "needs" and of the driving powers that result in cultural life, the needs can surely be a community affair as well. That a separation between economic and cultural creators is required, and furthermore that within each "rank" a further differentiation into various vocations is required, can be rendered understandable only by the real limitation of human personality, its powers and talents.[253]

---

252. [*Remedium* is Latin for "remedy."]

253. [The term "required" *(nötig)* is meant in an absolute phenomenological sense. Stein does not deny that social and economic inequalities occur for historical reasons. But those inequalities cannot be understood as necessary. They are understood precisely as contingent upon historical factors that affect individual human beings, such as having grown up in disadvantaged circum-

Now where the state must reckon with such qualities of its members, it is also within the sense of state that they form a community with vocationally ranked segmentation. The state's existence is tied to their being able to satisfy their needs in the framework of the state or at least—as far as aid from outside is necessary—through its mediation and not by depending on foreign powers. [Some factors are not up to the state.] What kind of economic labor there is, how the labor is divided up, what proportion of the people is absorbed in it (the Platonic "third rank")—this depends mostly upon conditions that the state does not control (like climate, the quality of the soil, and the like). Whenever economic and cultural life does not regulate itself in a way that corresponds to the state's interests, the state sees itself as required to intervene. Nevertheless it's obvious that *that* kind of "segmentation by status" is rooted primarily in the community founding the state and not in its own fabric. If the state bothers about it or makes provision that everything will function within its realm in a way that corresponds to the interests of the community (just as with concern for a sufficient number of inhabitants), the state does not immediately assure the preservation of sovereignty (as with the maintenance of the law), but rather [the state assures only], so to speak, the material basis for sovereignty, that which in fact makes sovereignty possible. This is what Aristotle had in view with his *autarchy* (which is to be inferred from books 6 and 7 of his *Politics).*[254] "Self-sufficiency" means factual independence from all foreign powers which is necessary so that the claim to rule cannot be disputed.

"Agencies" and "functions" are built in to the state organism

---

stances. The only necessary inequalities of rank are those that reflect innate differences in personal abilities, Stein argues. Therefore, socio-economic classes are not a necessary feature of the state. "Class warfare" occurs only as an unfortunate historical accident; it is not the essential driving force of history. See below.]

254. [Aristotle's account of autarchy or self-rule was discussed above in Part I §1.b. The *Politics* is a classic work of political theory by this Greek philosopher of the fourth century B.C.E.]

in a variety of ways, to which correspond a variety of postures of individuals toward the state. We already said earlier that not all individuals living in the state are "carriers" of the life of the state, nor in its interest must they be so. The labor of the "working classes," without which the state would be an empty form, can be accomplished in such a way as is necessary for giving the state a solid basis, without bringing those who accomplish that labor into league with the state. Conscious self-integration into the whole and a feeling of responsibility for it are imperative only for conducting [the affairs] of state.[255] With the executive agencies, dutiful commitment to the office suffices; the whole and the significance for the whole of the agency in question need not be perceived or have motivating power.

Now how did the distribution of the various necessary functions among the individuals come about? There are various possibilities.[256] Separation into classes is not an unqualified necessity. Conceivably you could have a political system in which the workers simultaneously participate in the formation of the state's will and bear responsibility for the execution of state decisions and ordinances. The individuals must then allocate their energies to the various functions. The extent to which this is possible in practice, and the way in which the form and the

---

255. [In other words, it doesn't matter to the state as such whether working-class persons are conscious of what their labor means to the state. The state requires such consciousness only in its political leaders. Stein refrains from saying whether she considers this a good thing or a bad thing, as she descriptively explores state phenomena. Her arguments contrast with the very different account offered by the Marxist theory of her day, in which the consciousness of the working classes was a key factor.]

256. [The question seems to be a historical one, but a phenomenological answer is given. Stein is concerned to establish logical criteria for understanding and evaluating the various historical accounts of the origin of the state that have been proposed by economists and political scientists. She is not attempting to do historical research herself.]

business of government are designed in accordance with it, are going to depend upon the quality of the land and of the inhabitants, and on their reciprocal determination. If economic life places very strong demands on the working energy of individuals, this could mean that they are entirely absorbed in it and have nothing more left over for the business of state.

Conversely the management of the state, which we now imagine to be consolidated in the hands of one or a few human beings, can influence the land and the inhabitants so as to rearrange them and thereby make possible an alteration of the form of government as well. The ruler could use state organization of educational matters to get the "citizens of the state" to open their eyes to the life of the state and their importance in it, and they would learn to orient their labor around that [insight]. Furthermore, he could let the economy be taken over by the state, using rational organization, technical aids, and the like to bring it about that less [working] energy is devoured by the economy and more becomes available for allotment to the life of the state.

Finally, it would be conceivable—as Plato depicts it, as he tries to show in what manner his "best state" would be allowed to realize itself—that an enlightened monarch would have a select group trained for the various functions of the state up to [but not including] state leadership, and in that way would prepare the ground for the transformation of the form of government.

h) The influence of the theory of the state upon the shaping of the state

This leads us to the question of how the theory of the state and the shaping the state—policy—are connected with one another.[257] Plato's *Republic* is the classic example of a theory of

---

257. "Policy" can have a threefold sense. It can signify the totality of state actions, and then it includes the second, narrower sense of policy as self-configuration of the state. The third meaning has to do not with actions of the state itself, but rather with efforts of single persons and groups to give the state a certain configuration or to extort certain acts.

the state that would like to gain influence in shaping the reality through the ideal.[258] The image of the state as it's supposed to be is set forth so that those who are situated in political life can now form the real state accordingly. But even if the doctrine of the state is not oriented in regard to practical policy from the outset, but rather tends only to ground what the sense of state is, it can exert a very strong effect upon the factual development [of the state].

Contract theory lets the state be grounded upon an agreement between governors and the governed (or among the governed with one another and then between them and the governmental authority to which they submit themselves). Contract theory has awakened the wish now actually to attribute the life of enduring states, or even states comprehended as emerging, to such a contract, and has led to the development of modern constitutional states.

The doctrine of natural law, going hand in hand with contract theory, would design the state by starting with the isolated individual. It would introduce the doctrine of "human rights and civil rights," which would be made operative in opposition to the state. Those rights would be the basis on which you would sometimes demand and even achieve a limitation of the state's sphere of influence, and sometimes encumber it with new functions in the interest of individuals (like social welfare and the like). Here is also a root of the democratic demand for participation of everyone in the life of the state, which has became a very great influence upon the development of modern states.

We are interested here only in the question in principle: how far can such a theory go in its influence upon the shaping of the state? If someone goes about putting a perverse theory of the state into practice, then certainly it does no damage to the *idea* of the state. Yet it exposes the prevailing states to the risk of a gradual

---

258. [The *Republic* is a Greek classic work of political theory. The title by which it is known in German is *Staat*, "State." See note 251 above.]

decomposition. If the "rights" of individuals are made out to be valid over against the state, then that signifies a challenge to sovereignty. And as soon as you try to force their recognition you're working toward the destruction of the state. (Those "rights," according to their main substance, are not grounded on legal norms but on *ethical* norms—whether on norms obtaining truly or allegedly is something that would have to be checked out in individual cases. It would be conceivable for the defense of those norms[259] to justify the destruction of any state that violated them. But you cannot make ethical norms into the content of a right[260] that would have to be imposed upon the state by another power.)

Ethical norms are to be reconciled with omnipotence of the state only in this form: that the state itself makes them the content of its law and limits itself in their favor. This self-limitation, arising with respect to norms other than legal norms, is to be distinguished from the one mentioned earlier, the self-limitation that is demanded by the idea of law itself. In reference to the latter, Jellinek is correct to say: "Such a self-limitation is not optional, which means it is not left up to the discretion of the state whether it wishes to exercise it at all."[261] The state, in making law, imposes the responsibility of observing the law not only upon the individuals and groups that belong to the state, but upon itself as well, and so upon its law-making agency. Nor may law be violated by the state's central will; the state's will can only rescind a law. Any exemption of the state from the obligation of observ-

---

259. [Literally, "their defense" *(ihre Verfechtung)*. The possessive pronoun probably refers to "norms," but grammatically could just as well refer to "rights" in both this and the following two sentences.]

260. [*Recht,* "right," can also mean "law."]

261. See Jellinek, *Allgemeine Staatslehre,* p. 386. [In quoting Jellinek, Stein made a minor change in the order of the words. It does not affect the meaning.]

ing the law it makes would annul the idea of law and along with it the idea of the state itself.[262]

Thus, out of the state's legal regulations there arise not only duties for individuals and claims that are intended by the content of the legal regulations, but also the claim to be treated in accordance with the operative law, a claim grounded in the pure form of law-making. However that general claim is not one that is definite in content. You can't deduce from it any "civil rights" obtaining *a priori* and binding for all empirical states regardless of their respective fabric. Consequently, what was said concerning the extra-legal character of the content of ethical norms[263] still holds.

Subversion of the state can originate not only with those who place demands upon the state in the name of individuals, but also with those who are agents of the state and especially with the leaders of the state. One instance in which that occurs—as we already saw—is when they themselves do not respect the law of the state. For obedience "is the complement of the civil authority, without which it is not able to exist."[264] Any violation of the law that remains unpunished is documentation of the powerlessness of the state, even if it comes from the ruler or from some individual involved in the government. And therefore it is at the same time a provocation to further breaches of the civil order.

It's a further endangerment of the state if its representatives

---

262. [In other words, the very idea of a state that violates its own laws is a self-contradictory idea, and cannot be rationally entertained. If real states are observed in the act of violating their own laws, then there must be a breakdown of perception somewhere. They may be bogus states, or perhaps the agents of the state who violate the law are not properly authorized to act on behalf of the state, or they overstep the terms of their authorization.]

263. [Literally, "their content" or "its content" *(ihres Inhalts)*. The context suggests that the possessive pronoun refers back to "ethical norms." However grammatically it could refer to any of several other nouns.]

264. See Jellinek, *Allgemeine Staatslehre,* p. 426.

become active in areas that are in principle off-limits to it. While the state does not reach into religious life itself, the state has the capability of putting a stop to expressions of religious life. But this damming up of a current whose source cannot be plugged up makes the current turn against the artificial barriers. And if it manages to break through them, then with that a breach is likewise made in the civil authority. Thus every time the state oversteps its authority, it arouses countervailing forces that threaten to destroy the civil authority itself. Conversely, a self-limitation not required by the idea of the state can lead to "moral victories" that secure the existence of the state.

Finally, it's a threat to the concrete pattern of the state if those who happen to be in power make a principle out of the preservation of the state order that obtains, or the introduction of a new one constructed purely theoretically, and try to enforce that principle even if the actual condition of the material foundations of the state in question makes a change necessary or goes against the planned change, as the case may be. For example, if the complexity of economic relationships renders it impossible in practice to manage them from a central point, then the maintenance or introduction of such a [centralized] system leads to the breakdown of the economy and endangers the substance of the state.

It's an especially serious situation for the state if different theories are fighting over it and trying to gain influence over it. Indeed, all fighting among political parties is an attempt to get control of the leadership of the state in order to model it as they see fit. Even if no well developed theory of the state is the dominant ideal, but special-interest groups are wrangling with one another for control, then within that very attempt by the private interests to advance their views on the issue of the configuration of the state there lies a quite definite view of the state (about which they don't even need to be clear) and it's surely a particularly dangerous view. Now for example, in a parliamentarily organized state, if different theories of the state take over the rudder with the change of parties, the downfall of the state can be brought about (according to its external aspect) systematically in a lawful way and without breaking the law.[265]

There's a corrective against all of these possible destructive influences of political theory, and it lies in the power of *ratio*, which the real relations themselves bear within themselves.[266] Every legal arrangement that offends against this *ratio* instead of taking it into account must be prepared for reality to resist it and run its course with constant breaches of the legal order. Certainly a disruption of the operations of the state is present here as well. It is a condition in which the commonwealth lingers on without a fixed civil arrangement. But for as long as the commonwealth persists, you may look for it to take on the form of the state once more. But if on the other hand the material basis upon which the political system was resting collapses (maybe at first while maintaining the formal legal order), then you must regard its downfall as sealed. Anything left over is spoils for a conqueror who wishes to take possession of it for himself, and raw material for another state to which it can be annexed.

---

265. It should not be asserted that therefore this is the necessary consequence of the parliamentary system. [The competing political "theories" could be termed "ideologies."]

266. [*Ratio* is Latin for "reasoning." Here it is recommended as preferable to the coercive measured discussed above; see note 248. The phenomenologist turns to the realm of ideas, an objective and unchanging realm, to counteract problems arising from the conflict of ideologies, which emerge historically. Stein perhaps has chosen the Latin term in order to avoid association with the idealism of Immanuel Kant and his well known critiques of reason *(Vernunft)*. The term *ratio* also connotes proper relationships in formal sciences such as logic and mathematics. In the classical tradition of Western philosophy prior to Kant, the human mind was deemed to be actively receiving reality when such relationships were known, without being their inventor or source.]

II. The state from perspectives of value

We hesitated to tackle the problem of the state's value and "legitimacy" before establishing, through an examination free of value perspectives, what the state really is. But that was supposed to be only a deferral and not a fundamental negation of the whole question. In principle, every being is a possible bearer of value and is not exhaustively discussed if its value is left out of consideration.[267]

The question of the legitimacy of any pattern makes sense only if its being, or its being just this way, is in our hands and is a possible target of the will. This requirement is to be regarded as fulfilled for the concrete state in a certain sense. Even if it doesn't depend completely upon the pleasure of one individual or of individuals in general whether a state emerges and is preserved or destroyed, or which [course of] development it takes, the state is still tied to the activity of individuals in regard to its existence and its quality. That means the state is dependent on the fact that individuals offer themselves as its agents or recognize it. This is the reason why the annihilation of the state and the condition of statelessness—anarchy—is a possible target of willing. Is it a desirable target or a reprehensible one? This question is answered simultaneously with the question of the justification of the state. But that justification is to be assessed when you know the value of the state and its relation to other values, which it can conflict with or be of importance for in some respect.

What is the sense of the question of the value of the state? This must be clarified first. It's a different question if we ask

---

267. [Stein differs from most phenomenologists in her insistence upon this technical point. She holds that the constitution of an object for consciousness includes the constitution of its value, and neither one determines the other. Thus the sense of state does not guarantee the legitimacy of state; in other words, "bad state" is not a contradiction in terms, nor is "good state" redundant.]

whether a concrete state pattern could be or must be a carrier of value, or whether we ask about the value "of the state." The second is the real question of principle: *is there any value to the state as such,* that is, to the ontic fabric that we were trying to work out in Part I? If that question can be answered affirmatively, then it is right *a priori* for there to be states in the world (or, of course, *wrong a priori* if the value that attaches to the state as such is a negative one). And now there's a value to these concrete patterns on the ground of the fact that they are states. If it turns out in a particular case that a state is not a carrier of such a value, then factors other than its fabric as a state must account for that. Those factors must be responsible for the fact that the value which it must have as a state is in fact suspended.

On the other hand: if the state as such should turn out to be a value-neutral pattern, that would still not say that concrete states could not be carriers of values on the basis of other compositional factors. The possibility of harboring value in that way[268] could be left open by the fabric of the state. The existence of states would then not be "justified" through reference to state fabric as such, yet neither would it be proven "wrong."[269]

These different possible meanings of the question of the value of the state must be kept in view as we set about examining this question.

§1. Significance of the state
for the individuals who belong to it

All theories that derive the state from the individual grant to it the significance that the individuals "get along better" in a state than when they are isolated or even when they live in a commu-

---

268. [Literally, "such a possible value-holding-ness" *(Werthaftigkeit).*]

269. [Stein was aware of extreme Marxist and anarchist arguments which asserted that the state as such was a bad thing and must be done away with. She disagrees. The fact that this or that concrete state may be evil does not prove that all states are evil just because they are states. See note 236, above.]

nity organized in some other way than as a state. Does that count as a justification? In any [given] concrete state it depends, first, on whether that's factually correct, and second, on what this "getting along better" means and whether this itself is to be regarded as something valuable. For the state as such, however, it depends on whether there's a place for the value in question within its fabric.

"Getting along better" can mean that the *necessities of life* of the individuals can be satisfied better in the state because of the regulated division of labor and that their life is better secured in the face of danger than it would be outside of the state. The state would then be an institution standing in the service of *values of life* and therefore useful.[270] The state as such is a possible carrier of this utility value. That means the idea of the state does not prescribe, but also does not exclude, that this value [i.e., utility for life] is realized in concrete state patterns. Whether or not that is factually the case in an empirical state depends upon *its* quality and upon that of the individuals who belong to it. Conceivably you could have individuals for whom—from the standpoint of utility—the state would be superfluous. And on the other hand, you could have states whose institutions do more to destroy life values than to further them, and that thus are to be designated as harmful. Therefore a justification in principle is not possible in this way.

A further attempt to justify the state can be made in the name of the *mental development* of individuals. Especially if the state frees up the higher powers by organizing the lower activities. And because by organizing the higher powers the state makes possible a production of mental goods that can come into existence only in this way.[271] Here as well, the state as such merely leaves the

---

270. On the concept of utility and on the doctrine of value in general, see Max Scheler, *Formalism in Ethics.* [Stein cites a 1916 German edition. The first part of Scheler's *Ethics* had appeared in 1913 in the *Jahrbuch,* and Stein read it during her first year of studies at Göttingen. See note 58 above.]

271. [The last few lines are not complete sentences in the original German, as Stein adopts a conversational tone.]

possibility open for the concrete states once again. Then in principle it is not to be rejected out of hand that the mental life could develop just as well or better without state regulation as it does with it. And conceivably there are states that do more to destroy mental values than to help produce them.[272]

§ 2. State and justice

It's time to ask whether the realization of values isn't specially assigned to the state on the grounds of its proper fabric, and which values we're talking about here. After what we've established about the connections between state and law—that the law has need of a law-making subject in order to become an operative law, and that making law is specific to the state—it would be easy to see the "vocation" of the state in the realization of the law. Of course, "the law" here no longer means the empty form of right. (It would be absurd to specifically give the state what its life as state consists of [already].) Rather, here "the law" means plain right relations materially fulfilled.[273] It's up to "the law" to say whether that which is right, in and of itself, is also recognized as a law operative within the realm where it rules.[274] The extent to which a state is a "rightful" state or not is measured according to whether its positive law is a "right" law or not, that is, whether its positive law concurs with pure law or not.[275]

The *idea of justice* is related to the pure law. Where the pure

---

272. [*Geistig,* "mental," can also mean "spiritual" throughout the preceding paragraph. The term covers what we would call cultural and intellectual affairs.]

273. ["Plain right relations" *(Rechtsverhalte)* and "pure law" *(reines Recht)* received a technical exposition above, Part I, §2.a.]

274. [*In seinem Herrschaftsbereich,* "within the realm where it rules," is literally "in its sovereign territory."]

275. [Terms used here are cognates: *Recht,* "law" or "right"; *richtig,* "rightful" or "correct"; *gerecht,* "just"; and *Gerechtigkeit,* "justice." The similarities of sound and spelling in German make the argument all the more compelling.]

law is in force, there "justice reigns." Justice is a value-predicate that on the one hand can be attributed to an operative legal order and expresses its concurrence with the pure law, and on the other hand can be attributed to the subjects who work together in the realization of that legal order in that they posit it, or recognize and obey it. In principle it would be conceivable that no violation would be committed against the pure law even if there were no state to secure its effectiveness. The state is required, in the interests of the materialization of the law, only to the extent that individuals lack insight into the relations of pure law or lack the will to act according to them.

Therefore the state is not a *conditio sine qua non*[276] for the realization of justice. On the other hand—as we saw—the idea of the state does not exclude [the possibility] that the positive law made by a state deviates from the pure law, and is "unjust." Indeed, that can be required in the concrete case by the sense of the state.[277] Thus it won't do to assign to the state the realization of justice as the vocation prescribed for it by its idea. Nor is the state to be justified in principle through reference to that value.

§ 3. Significance of the state for the community as such and especially for the ethnic community

Suppose someone raised the objection that the life of the community, purely as such, is of value. That still would not justify the state in principle, because it is not essential for the community as such to assume the form of the state. To organize as a state is required in the interests of the community only to the extent that community life is endangered by impulses that live within the individuals. Even from the standpoint of the community, the

---

276. [*Conditio sine qua non* is Latin for "condition without which not" or "necessary condition."]

277. [In other words, in some concrete circumstances it might be unjust to have any civil laws at all; no possible form of state law could be just in those circumstances. Such circumstances are possible in principle.]

justification would be a merely factual one, which means it would consist only in the evidence that the individuals are in fact so conditioned and that the state in question at any given time is able to guarantee the correction of this condition.

In earlier reflections, we hit upon yet another significance of the state order. We saw that in particular the ethnic community, as a culturally productive personality, calls for organization as a state, and indeed does so not merely because—like any community—it has need of protection against tendencies disruptive of community, but because beyond that its distinctiveness as a trading and producing community makes necessary a fixed system for that trade and production. A circle of persons who live in ongoing contact can manage without such a system. In this case, each one can survey the whole and the significance of the discrete members in the make-up of the whole, and can behave accordingly. It's different if the community can no longer be taken in at a glance by the discrete members—as is in fact the case with the numbers necessary for the scope of an ethnic group. Here, institutions become necessary, at least those which make possible an overview of the needs and powers of the community for certain agencies to be developed specifically for that, and a fixed system for the execution of the collective decisions and transactions. This systematization and institutionalization is a matter for a system of positive law.

As to the content of that system, there's nothing to certify in advance that it must concur with the pure law, since after all the content is prescribed for the legal system by other points of view. (Presently we are coming to discuss the possibility of a conflict.) The value of the legal system is measured not according to the idea of justice, but according to the development of the community life, which the system serves. Community as such has a value all its own; and the ethnic community as a culturally productive personality has inherent value above and beyond that.[278] The state,

---

278. [Literally, "To community as such and beyond that, to ethnic community as a culture-creating personality, accrues a particular value."]

which with its legal system is placed in the service of the community's life, does not *create* that value but only *helps* to realize it. The value that accrues to the state in return, provided that it does this, is not an inherent value but merely a derivative value.

You can claim that "the state" is a carrier of the value under consideration here only if "state" is understood to mean not the formal fabric but rather the concrete pattern of the state that encompasses the ethnic community too. The values at stake here are "personality values." Just as each individual person is a carrier of an irreplicable value proper to herself alone, so too is each "state personality."

And with this, the question of the justification of the state is placed upon a new ground. For anyone who is vividly feeling the value of a political system (thinking here namely of someone who is a citizen of it), this problem of whether he should regard the political system as entitled to exist is just as unlikely to crop up as is the question of whether a person whom he loves is entitled to exist. Everything with value exhibits its right to exist, in that it makes its intrinsic value felt.[279]

But that doesn't resolve all the issues. Since values can emerge in competition, and since one value may through its realization exclude the realization of others, you always have to examine, regardless of what values are in themselves, the extent to which they can be allowed to hold their own over against other values, or the extent to which it is right for them to impose

---

279. [Literally, "makes its intrinsic value feel-able" *(fühlbar)*. Feeling includes more than emotion and sensation, in Stein's philosophy. Feeling is the way in which we experience the flow of our inner life as we think, plan, understand, and so forth. The German word for "empathy," *Einfühlung,* includes all those activities. This was the topic of Stein's doctoral dissertation *On the Problem of Empathy,* CWES 3. In feeling, we get reliable knowledge of something through the way in which it affects us inwardly. Value is perceived and known primarily through feeling.]

themselves at the expense of other values. First of all, it would be conceivable for the personality value of the prevailing concrete state pattern to turn out to be in conflict with justice, the value that is referred to the state and its fabric for its realization. For example, a state could regard itself as forced, in the interests of its development, to dissociate itself from responsibilities that it entered into (financial covenants with regard to its citizens, treaties with other states, and the like). Refusing to satisfy a claim to which you committed yourself by a promise is always a violation of the law. However, that refusal can be offered in the interest of a higher value. When that case arises for the state is not something that can be determined by any general law. There are general laws of precedence, but the correct decision concerning the relationship of concrete values standing in conflict at any given time will depend, as a rule, on a whole series of such laws, whose possible combinations in practice are not to be anticipated.

§4. The state and moral values

The preceding considerations bring up the question of whether, and to what extent, ethical norm-setting involves the state.[280]

---

280. [Literally, "whether and to what extent the state is affected by ethical norm-setting." In German as in English, a distinction is made between "ethical" *(ethisch)* and "moral" *(sittlich),* although the concepts are related. See Stein's excursus, below. Morality has to do with right action. Ethics has to do with systematic, rigorous reflection about the grounds for judging whether an action is right or wrong. Stein customarily treats the idea of the state as a norm, that is, as the criterion for determining what is possible and proper for those concrete states that actually exist. But the idea of the state is a logical norm, not an ethical norm. Stein has argued that the state as such has no value in its own right, but can acquire value to the extent that the state serves the interests of persons and communities. The discussion enters the realm of comparative values here. The ideal, phenomenological perspective now must broaden out to include another discourse, that of moral value.]

a) Morality and law

Ethical values are personal values. They attach to the essential substance of the person and her ways of comporting herself.[281] They show up in her comportment toward values of all kinds: in how she allows herself to be filled up by a value, how she takes a stance toward it, the values to which she gives precedence before others, and those for which she decides to take action.

Besides that, you can claim that there is ethical significance to what we designate as *"morally right."* This is a predicate of a certain state of affairs. ("That the needy are helped," or, "that X.Y. has declined to take part in a vile deed"—this is right.) Rightness and ethical person-values are not unconnected with one another. It's always persons, and persons' ways of comporting themselves, that form the objective material of those states of affairs for which the claim can be made that they are morally right. [But] moral rightness has nothing to do with the law, in the sense established so far. If I refuse help to someone who needs it, when I am able to help him, then that's "wrong" in the moral sense but not in the legal sense. The realization of states of affairs known as morally right is assigned to persons as a moral duty.

Does an ethical norm differ from a legal norm, and if so, how? Ethical states of affairs and states of affairs of pure law *subsist* in the same manner, without having to be made operative.[282] They are distinguished only by their *content:* in

---

281. [*Person* is grammatically feminine in German, but the sense is gender inclusive. It would be quite correct to substitute masculine pronouns in translating this passage.]

282. [That is, they do not come about through acts of law-making at some point in time. Stein regards both pure law and ethical rightness as matters of objective fact, which do not change from culture to culture or from time to time.]

accordance with the objectivities that are foundational for them. Persons and personal manners of comportment play a role for both; but there are different constituents of the person, and of the manners of comportment corresponding to the person, that come into consideration with the one and with the other. Of moral relevance are the uniqueness of soul of the person along with those aspects of life where it plays itself out: qualities of soul, dispositions, emotional attitudes, and the like.[283]

All of that is legally indifferent. Humility and pride, love and hate, admiration and contempt are not significant for any legal relation. The only issue here is the freedom of the person, and indeed those free acts that are *legally effective*. Legal efficacy means that something arises out of the acts of the person, or even that something is eradicated through them, which possesses its existence separately from the person. This includes all positive law, which is put into effect through law-making acts; the claim that arises from the act of promising; the ownership that is created, for example, through a transfer (thinking here of the *legal form* of the property, not of the extra-legal *matter,* considered in itself, that enters in to that form); the guilt that is brought into the world by a criminal deed and calls for punishment as a claim calls for satisfaction, and so forth. All of those are instances of specifically legal objectivities, and in conjunction with the legally effective acts they form the objective material for the state of affairs of pure law.

The specifically legal objectivities have no analog in the area of ethics. And to the extent that free acts play a role in that area, they do so as acts of the person, not as producers of such objectivities.

---

283. [Once again, German adjectival forms of "soul" are used: *seelische Eigenart,* "uniqueness of soul," and *seelische Qualitäten,* "qualities of soul." Though English needs the noun, it does not appear in German. For the meaning of *Seele,* "soul," see above, Part I, §3.d, and note 219.]

Excursus on guilt[284]

The situation is obscured by the fact that many times we operate with equivocal expressions that apply equally well to an ethical or a legal data set. Thus, "guilt" in the ethical sense is to be thoroughly distinguished from guilt in the legal sense.[285] The latter is something that exists in the world as a result of a criminal act—detached from the transgressive deed and from its perpetrator. The former [i.e., guilt in the ethical sense] is a tainting of the soul and has no sense at all apart from the person who has "taken it upon herself"; and on the other hand it can obtain without the commission of any criminal deed, even though it is tied to an offense. We could separate it from guilt in the legal sense by designating it as *sin.* Even here, you can't avoid a certain ambiguity. That is to say, sinfulness can be a quality of the soul before and independently of any actively wicked stirring (*peccatum originalis).*[286] Conversely, you can talk about sin (=guilt) only in

---

284. [At this point in the text, Stein inserted a footnote that runs on for six pages in the German and has footnotes of its own. Comprising a short essay in its own right, this material may have been drafted in response to the 1919 article on punishment by Dietrich von Hildebrand cited within it. At any rate, it apparently was inserted after the main text was written, with no attempt at integration into the main argument. It is presented here as an excursus or digression within the text. The main discussion picks up again below.]

285. [*Schuld,* "guilt," can also mean "debt." The choice of term depends upon the context.]

286. [*Peccatum originalis* is the Latin term for "original sin." Stein is using this well known doctrine as an example to illustrate her point. She does not intend to offer a theological exposition of this concept here. In the next sentence, *peccatum actuale* is Latin for "actual sin." Actual sins are those which someone commits during his or her lifetime. Original sin is the condition common to all human beings (except for Jesus and Mary, according to Catholic teaching) and is attributed to the disobedience of Adam and Eve as narrated in

the case of a *peccatum actuale*. We can set aside *peccatum originalis* entirely here, because there's no danger of confusion with guilt in the legal sense. Besides that, we're leaving aside [the issues of] what sin means religiously and where it was first instantiated.[287]

In order to define guilt correctly in the legal sense, we must now adduce the relations of *positive* law, which we have not yet considered in this context. Law-making acts have the power to generate legal patterns, even where you've got no legally effective acts of the kind that must "really" be present—according to pure law, that is—for such a pattern to be able to emerge. The law-making authority determines that any transgression of its precepts has to count as a guilt. This determination need not be expressly performed and pronounced. It is implied in the law-making as such. What is brought about by this is that anyone who disobeys a precept of the legitimate authority burdens himself with guilt and deserves punishment, even if what he did is not a crime in the sense of pure law.

However, a distinction obtains between the legal patterns that arise from legally effective acts according to pure law and those that are produced by making a law. Enacted laws take effect only in the region that the law-making authority has appropriated as its sphere of sovereignty, and the patterns that are produced by those laws are bound like them to that sphere. Beyond that sphere they are nothing. "Pure" law patterns are free of any such bounded-

---

the Bible. Christians believe that Jesus, though he was personally sinless, took it upon himself to pay for the guilt of all human sins.]

287. [Literally, "wherein its sense was first fulfilled." This is the phenomenological way of referring to the point in time when a hypothetical possibility first became a reality; that is, when some thing or event or state of affairs came into being for which the concept had always been available. Technically, that concept would not entail the existence of a mind to think it up; its possibility is purely a matter of logic. In other words, "sin" is a logical corollary of "free will" and "purposeful creation," by the very meanings of the terms, whether or not creation of such a will actually has occurred.]

ness. This might become a little clearer if we look at the *destruction* of legal patterns instead of their production. A debt that obtains according to pure law can be declared null and void by the positive law. Then the debt is wiped out in the sphere of the positive law but not disposed of entirely.[288]

Concerning guilt in the sense now unambiguously established, we said that it calls for punishment. Guilt is not *obliterated* by the punishment, which means the punishment is not capable of annihilating the guilt as though it had never been there. What is achieved by the execution of the punishment is a *cancellation* of the guilt and thereby an obliteration of the element of disquiet that is agitating for a further occurrence. The equilibrium of the world that was disturbed by the guilt is restored by the punishment.[289]

The *sin* is not affected at all by the punishment; the punishment does not penetrate into the sphere of the person in any way. What sin calls for is not punishment but *repentance,* which means something that happens within the soul, just like sin itself.[290]

---

288. [Literally, "not altogether excised from the world."]

289. [Medieval authors like Anselm of Canterbury (1033-1109) regarded the universe as a hierarchical moral order whose equilibrium was upset by unjust acts. This philosophical notion entered into St. Anselm's interpretation of the work of Christ as substitutionary atonement, and Anselm's theological opinion in turn influenced Christian teaching in the West. Stein may have encountered this idea in either context: theology or the history of philosophy.]

290. [In other words, the remedy for sin must be the kind of occurrence that takes effect at the core of the person, in the arena of free decision. Stein stipulated above that the term "sin" is lifted out of its religious context and used here only as a familiar example to illustrate an argument about law as such. At this point, then, no religious or theological meaning should be read into the text. Stein is working in the area of philosophical anthropology. For her account of the various regions within human being, with their differing accessibility, see her earlier treatise "Sentient Causality," CWES 7: 2-128. The notion of "soul" in the present treatise stands in continuity with that account, but has undergone further development. See note 222, above.]

Punishment means nothing there except insofar as it can be a *motive* that impels toward repentance. (This possibility in principle is to be distinguished from the factual question of whether the human being is capable of such repentance on his own.) Sin as defilement of the soul can be wiped out by perfect repentance. What cannot be wiped out, but can only be "forgiven," is the crime that was once committed.

It's easy to overlook the distinction between guilt and sin because of the connection that obtains between the two. The criminal act with which the guilt arises is simultaneously an event within the soul, the start of a *peccatum actuale*.[291] Yet we have already seen that sin without guilt is possible.[292] But the reverse is not the case (*scilicet* as long as it's a matter of pure guilt[293]). Certainly it could be that guilt and sin stand in a very different relationship to one another—thus with different possible motives that could lead to one and the same transgressive action, or if the actual result of the action diverges from the intended result as with "negligent homicide." But if the realization of a negatively valued state of affairs is imposed purely as a causal result of an action, without being the deliberate goal or even being foreseen only as a possible result, then not only is there no sin, there's not

---

291. [*Peccatum actuale* is Latin for "actual sin." Stein continues to use the theological category as an illustration. See note 286, above.]

292. [For example, it is possible for sin to remain subjectively after guilt has been canceled objectively. The social act that wipes out guilt or debt, really and objectively, still does not reach deeply enough into the core of the person to affect the soul, according to Stein's argument. As a second example, Stein may also be thinking of the classic Christian doctrine of "original sin." Here, sin mars the soul of the unbaptized person even before any guilt is incurred through evil actions. Stein herself had not yet been baptized when she wrote these words.]

293. [*Scilicet* is Latin for "that is to say." "Pure guilt" would be incurred under "pure law" and so would always be accompanied by defilement of the soul of the one who chose to violate the law.]

even any guilt. The relationships are otherwise if it's a matter of a guilt based on positive law. Such a guilt can be without any ethical significance.

Our comments on guilt and punishment disagree on a few points with those expressed by Dietrich von Hildebrand in his treatise "On the Essence of Punishment."[294] These disagreements, in my opinion, are based on this: that the distinction between the ethical sphere and the legal sphere, which is the main point for us, is not maintained by him and so is not thought through in its significance for the problem at hand. This shows up, for example, in the differentiation between expiatory punishment and absolute punishment. Expiatory punishment—according to Hildebrand— makes sense only where the sinner has insight into his guilt and regrets it, and then the punishment enables the sin to be wiped out. On the other hand, absolute punishment comes to the fore where there's no remorse and therefore no "expiation," that is, no wiping out of the guilt, is possible. Then the guilt is not disposed of by the punishment. But the punishment does not become superfluous or senseless because of that. On the contrary, it becomes permanently necessary precisely in that way. The guilt of hardened sinners requires eternal punishment. [For Hildebrand] the punishing of guilt represents a value—entirely apart from wiping it out. (The value is analogous to that of rewarding merit.) Not to punish guilt would mean a new disvalue—in addition to the guilt.

It's easy to see that what is being described here transpires in two different spheres. The punishment as such is directed against the guilt, and what is going on inside of the originator of the guilt makes no difference for the punishment. The only qualification

294. Dietrich von Hildebrand, "Zum Wesen der Strafe," *Philosophisches Jahrbuch der Görresgesellschaft,* new year 1919. [Von Hildebrand (1898-1977) belonged to the Göttingen circle of phenomenologists along with Stein. His earlier work on ethics was cited in her *Philosophy of Psychology,* CWES 7. He would go on to become an influential moral theologian and ecclesiologist in the United States.]

needed is that the guilt can be assigned only through finding the personal originator of it (or, someone taking his place), and that it is he who "suffers the punishment." But what further emotional[295] effects the punishment has, or whether it is accepted as "justified" and the guilt is regretted (these two have a certain connection but need not necessarily be linked), has nothing further to do with the punishment as such.[296]

Expiation is a completely new process that can be combined with the process of punishment but signifies no differentiation of the punishment. Expiation is accomplished on the inside of the soul, like repentance, yet is to be distinguished from the latter. Repentance is directed toward the sinful condition of the soul. Expiation is directed toward the entirely definite and, so to speak, sharply outlined and tangible *peccatum actuale,* just as the punishment is directed toward the guilt graspable in a definite way.[297] Expiation is accomplished in that the sinner takes upon himself an entirely definite suffering or an exact performance through which the sin is supposed to be offset. The expiation may perhaps materially coincide with suffering the punishment. You expiate in that you "take upon yourself" the punishment inflicted.

---

295. [*Seelisch,* "emotional," is literally "soul-ish." These would be effects occurring within the core of the person. There is no adequate English translation.]

296. [The last two paragraphs are meant to summarize the position of von Hildebrand. Stein disagrees with this position and goes on to say why.]

297. [*Peccatum actuale* is Latin for "actual sin." See note 286, above. Stein applies the phenomenological notion of intentionality. Repentance and expiation are "intentional," in the technical sense, in that they are what they are precisely by referring to some other definite sense: that of the very specific sin or the very specific guilt, respectively. In other words, you must repent of, or expiate for, something in particular. It would make no sense to repent or expiate in general. Analogously, punishment must be "for" something in particular. Without a reference to a specific crime, it's not punishment but merely oppression or torture.]

But this is precisely where the contrast emerges so clearly. That punishment "be imposed" belongs necessarily to punishment. But that you "take it upon yourself" does not belong to punishment in any way. This "taking up" is to be completely separated from the "laying down" of punishment, unless its sense is not fully worked out. The imposition of punishment means— as already mentioned—only that the guilty one suffers and understands the suffering as punishment for the guilt. And this is possible even if he doesn't submit himself in any way but protests against it vehemently. The suffering is only an instrument for the punishment, and to be sure, the plain fact of the suffering no matter how it is experienced. But expiation is suffering,[298] and indeed a definite kind of suffering, born out of a heart disposed to be "ready to repent" and essentially presupposed for that, and bound up with operations of the heart that belong just as necessarily to this disposition.[299]

Now what is it that is gained through punishment, and what is gained through expiation? That which Hildebrand describes as the result of absolute punishment seems to me to paraphrase the result possible with punishment in general: the guilt is not wiped out but "it no longer cries out unto heaven." That which is effected by expiation is something analogous in its own sphere. The sin is not simply wiped out by expiation either. But the "stinger" is taken out of it. Just as the punishment re-establishes the equilibrium of the world that was disrupted by the guilt, so the expiation re-establishes the equilibrium of the soul that was disrupted by the sin. Yet the expiation presupposes that the sin is already rendered inoperative by remorse and repentance, which

---

298. In lieu of suffering, another positive action or performance can be considered expiation, as already anticipated, but then it must be accomplished in the same disposition of repentance.

299. [Literally, "But expiation is suffering, and surely a definite kind of suffering, born out of a soul-ish *(seelisch)* disposition of "repentance-readiness" essentially presupposed for that, and bound with soul-ish *(seelisch)* effects belonging just as necessarily thereto."]

means the sin is prevented from propagating further as unrepented sin does. And for this there is no analog in the area of guilt and punishment.

That clears up the distinction between punishment and expiation. Yet some doubt may still obtain regarding the character of guilt and punishment in pure law. Why is it—you well might ask—that the punishment must *affect* the guilty one (or, another "in his place")? Does this not point to an ethical significance for guilt?[300] Hildebrand speaks of a "guilt evil" and of a moral disvalue that attaches to guilt. Yet an important distinction is missing here too. Any guilt—as we said—to the extent that it does not owe its existence to an enactment of positive law, arises in connection with a moral lapse: whenever an unjust state of affairs is realized. The state of affairs is characterized as "unjust" and its realization as morally negative and therefore as sinful.

Yet neither the state of affairs nor the action through which it is realized is the guilt. The guilt came into the world through the realization of the unjust state of affairs and shares its matter with it. But the guilt has its own particular property: precisely the demand for a punishment through which it is "crossed out" but still not annihilated. The moral blemish that the person has incurred through the realization of the unjust state of affairs can be wiped out through repentance and remorse. The guilt, if it is crossed out by the punishment appropriate to it, no longer obtains but rather "has obtained." The unjust state of affairs obtains for all eternity, unaffected by punishment, remorse, repentance, or expiation. And that is precisely why the guilt can only be crossed out but not annihilated.

Nor does it change anything if the damage can be made good

---

300. [The question arises because Stein earlier had made a distinction between the legal and the ethical spheres. She argued above that punishment was an affair of the legal sphere, where the attitude of the punished one toward the punishment was irrelevant. Only in the ethical sphere were inner dispositions supposed to matter. Feeling affected by a punishment would seem to be an event transpiring within the person.]

again. That damage has been inflicted on someone, and it belongs to the matter of the unjust state of affairs, just as it belongs to the matter of the guilt. The unjust state of affairs and the guilt alike are independent of the one who had to suffer under them. The one affected can pardon the originator of his suffering, and for that, certainly, neither punishment nor repentance nor reparation is presupposed. Sin and guilt, like the unjust state of affairs, remain unaffected by the forgiveness. By the reparation, the suffering is taken away from the one affected. That is something to which he has a claim—a claim grounded in the guilt, to the extent that guilt was "guilt toward him." The claim is fulfilled and dissolved through the reparation. With that, the guilt ceases to be a guilt "toward anyone." But that still does not cross it out completely, because it has substance in itself, independently of the impact upon the victim. That substance is gotten at only by punishment, not by reparation. And these two are to be separated, even though occasionally the reparation can be imposed as a punishment. But nothing can touch the unjust state of affairs.

Distinctions analogous to those made for guilt and punishment are to be made for merit and reward. Someone who brings to realization a state of affairs recognized as morally right has "earned himself" merit. The merit does not coincide either with the state of affairs or with the morally worthy action; it is merely grounded in them. Merit *is due* a reward, just as guilt is due a punishment. For the originator [of the merit] there arises from it a claim to a reward.[301] The state of affairs to which the merit is tied knows no such demand for reward, no more than does the action of bringing it to realization. Just as you become guilty "toward someone," so do you make yourself "meritorious with regard to someone." A gain for someone is always bound up with merit. And the *"gaudens"* thereby becomes obligated for thank-

---

301. It is well to observe that here again we're dealing with legal contexts, not ethical ones. It is entirely compatible with the fact that a merit legally obtains, that it's negatively valued—considered ethically—to credit something to yourself as merit and levy a claim for a reward.

ing the originator of the merit.[302] This thanks, in turn, is not to be confused with the reward. The rewarding can take place when the one obliged to give thanks turns out not to be thankful, and vice versa. Yet it's also possible for the thanks to acquire the function of reward, to be "used" as reward, so to speak. If the rewarding has occurred, then the claim based upon the merit has found satisfaction, and the merit is on the books in a manner analogous to the guilt after the punishment.[303] However the state of affairs again still subsists unchanged.

Guilt and merit have a personal originator. They call for reward and punishment, and these must be "executed," which means that for their part they [too] refer back to a personal originator. *Who* is called upon to reward and to punish? The answer sounds different, depending on whether you're talking about "pure" guilt or guilt based on positive law. (The same goes for merit.) Guilt reckoned according to posited, statutory law[304] can be punished only by the law-making authority (or by agents empowered by it). The guilt is in existence because of that authority, just as the law-making authority determines which punishment corresponds to the guilt.[305]

---

302. [*Gaudens* is Latin for "the one rejoicing," or the beneficiary.]

303. [*Ad acta gelegt,* "on the books," is an idiom concocted out of the Latin phrase *agere lege,* "to take legal action," and the German verb *liegen,* "be placed." *Acta,* formed from the Latin past participle of *agere,* can mean "legal records." Although the Latin ablative *lege* and German participle *gelegt* are not related philologically, the similar sound allows Stein to emphasize the real, objective, and unchangeable character of merit and guilt. Once either is incurred it is a matter of record forever, even if subsequently canceled.]

304. [Literally, "the latter." The pronoun *diese* refers to "guilt based on positive law."]

305. [Literally, "to which it owes its existence, and it also determines simultaneously which punishment corresponds to it." The different cases of the German pronouns, together with the context, make the antecedents clear.]

In the other case, the guilty party can take upon himself the punishment that is imposed upon him by an earthly judge.[306] (With what right on the side of the earthly judge this occurs, remains to be discussed.[307]) But even if no earthly judge is found for him, even if no one knows his guilt, he can figure out what punishment is due him, and can either [1] interpret some misfortune that befalls him as a punishment for his guilt, or [2] impose upon himself a punishment that seems to him to be commensurate with the guilt. In the first case [1] it's completely obvious that *God* seems to him to be the punishing judge. Yet even if [2] he himself seeks out the punishment, he doesn't do this as a proper judge but rather on the basis of an alleged mandate coming from that which is entitled to punish him.[308] And if he takes upon himself a punishment that an earthly judge has imposed upon him, then that implies that he recognizes that judge as a representative of the real judge (provided that he's not just submitting to external coercion).

Because the maintenance of the order of the world, which

---

306. [This "other case" is that of guilt according to "pure law." This guilty party has done something that is wrong absolutely, even if there were no statutory law against it. The guilt would be in existence even without the statute. But in this example, the crime also happens to carry a penalty under statutory law. The "earthly judge" is the agent of the civil authority that made that law. This judge is "earthly" in contrast to the absolute reality of "pure law." The term "earthly" also suggests a contrast with "heavenly." The notion of God is introduced below, as an imagined agent of punishment.]

307. ["What right" could also be translated "what law," since *Recht* can mean either "right" or "law."]

308. [*Von seiten dessen, dem das Strafen zusteht,* "coming from that which is entitled to punish him," could be either impersonal or personal in German. Another possible translation is: "on the part of the one who is entitled to do the punishing." In the next sentence, the phrase "the real judge" implies that Stein sees a person behind "pure law," that absolute, impersonal distinction between right and wrong that obtains prior to and independent of any statutory law.]

comes to expression in the weighing of guilt and punishment, merit and reward, can be vested in no finite person by her inherent right, it is a matter for the lord of the world.[309] We concur with Hildebrand that punishment, according to its sense, points back at God as the ultimate originator. Yet Hildebrand goes a little too far when he says that—as soon as this context is no longer in view —any sense drops away from punishment, leaving it with only those functions that are non-essential to it and that play such a large role in modern criminal law: *vengeance* (through which the victim procures satisfaction for himself); *protection* (of the victim, or of those who are in danger of becoming victims of further injury); *reform* of the guilty party. None of those functions has anything to do with the specifically legal relations of guilt and punishment. Yet those specific legal relations can be known, and it's possible for an earthly judge to take upon himself their maintenance, without having insight into whom that maintenance is really vested in. And furthermore, the fact that punishment hints at a divine judge, in whom its execution is vested, changes nothing about the legal character of the punishment, nor does it shift the punishment into the field of the ethical.[310] We've got to

---

309. [The argument that Stein cites here is a variant of one of the standard "proofs of the existence of God," the so-called moral argument. Versions of this argument appear in the works of Immanuel Kant and John Henry Newman, both of whom were familiar to Stein. But here the argument is given a phenomenological twist. The reality of the pressure that we feel toward righting wrongs is such that even to feel this pressure is simultaneously to know that it must come from some source. This felt tendency toward rectifying imbalances of justice would be a kind of feelable "motivation" in the phenomenological technical sense of that term. This phenomenological version of the standard argument may have been suggested to Stein by the essay of Dietrich von Hildebrand cited above in note 294. However, she indicates in the next few sentences below that the argument does not prove the existence of God at all. For Kant's version of the moral argument, see *Critique of Practical Reason,* Book II, Chapter 2, sections 4 and 5. For Newman's, see J.H. Newman, *A Grammar of Assent,* edited by C.F. Harrold (New York: David McKay Co., 1947), 83-84.]

310. [See note 300, above, for the distinction between the legal and the ethical spheres.]

insist on that, despite all the connections with ethical findings.[311]

Apart from those connections, the regulations of *criminal statutory law* shed no light.[312] They are not oriented exclusively to the legal circumstances, but many times they are oriented to ethical findings as well. And they allocate punishment not by the guilt but by the sin (which can be supported on pedagogical grounds but not on legal ones).[313]

*

311. [Stein's disagreement with von Hildebrand is subtle but significant. She maintains that there's a sense to punishment within the impersonal legal sphere, quite apart from the personal ethical sphere governed by the "lord of the world," God. She imputes to von Hildebrand the view that to take God out of the picture is to wipe out the core sense of punishment. If von Hildebrand were correct, then our inner feeling of the necessity of punishment, its being *deserved*, would exhibit the reality of God. (And God would thereby be revealed precisely as punisher.) Stein argues to the contrary that the reality of God can indeed be bracketed—left out of consideration—with no loss in sense for punishment. Her argument defeats von Hildebrand's phenomenological version of the moral proof for the existence of God, without either affirming or denying the reality of God.]

312. [Literally: "the regulations of the *positive criminal law* work obscuringly," that is, have the effect of obscuring.]

313. The extent to which references to the moral law play a role even in our civil law is treated by Otto von Gierke, "Recht und Sittlichkeit," *Logos* 4/3 (1917): 211-264. We concur with him when he reciprocally delimits law and morality by the fact that they tie in to different spheres of the person *(an verschiedenen Personsphären anknüpfen).* What law is cannot be brought to perfect salience by von Gierke because he misses the distinction between pure law and positive law—with the acuteness of principle, at any rate. [Otto von Gierke joined with Edmund Husserl, Ernst Troeltsch, Max Weber, and several other leading scholars to sponsor the journal *Logos,* which billed itself as "an international journal for the philosophy of culture." Husserl had published important phenomenological work in vol. 1 this journal. This footnote within the longer footnote brings to a close Stein's excursus on guilt, and the main text resumes at this point.]

Within the ethical, we may very well find a parallel to the distinction between the pure and the positive law. There are states of affairs generally characterized as ethical which admit of being flipped over into norms. (It is right to help those in need.—You should help those in need.) These subsist as simple facts of value, *a priori,* without having to be posited and recognized. The same goes for simple facts of what should be done.[314] They can be rendered operative when they are made into the content of *legal* regulations (which is the case many times in the criminal statutory law). And they can also be rendered operative in yet another manner. Besides the ethical norms that obtain *a priori,* there is the *morality prevailing* at any given time (that is, defined temporally and spatially): views on that which is moral. Those can deviate from the just-so of ethics[315] obtaining *a priori,* in the same way that the positive law can deviate from the pure law. And there is a standardization of practical life through those views. The "prevailing" of the morality admits of comparison with the "being in effect" of the law, which means the "being in force" is congruent in the two cases.

However the *source* is otherwise. Morality cannot be *posited* like law. Morality mirrors back the *habitus* of soul of a commu-

---

314. [Stein appeals to the reader's basic insight into the independent reality of rightness, obligation, and the connection of the two. She uses the phenomenological term *Sachverhalt,* "state of affairs," in combination with the terms "value" and "should," producing new words that defy literal translation. See above, notes 77 and 78. The gist of her argument is that ethical rightness and moral obligation are objectively real and are also correlated with each other, point for point. Their substance both is and is knowable *a priori*—a Latin term with the technical meaning of "prior to" any particular experience or enactment, and in this case, prior to the making and recognizing of statutory laws. Yet Stein does not entirely repudiate moral relativism in what follows.]

315. [*Ethischen Sachverhalten,* "just-so of ethics," could also be translated "ethical state of affairs."]

nity of persons, its basic stance toward the world of values.[316] Just as the latter [stance] cannot be produced, changed, or abolished through free acts, neither can morality. [Yet] if the regulations of the positive law are, as to their content, opposed to the prevailing morality, then it's possible for that to bring about an alteration in the typical behavior of individuals in the area where the regulations are operative. And it's possible for a transformation of morality to set in on the basis of the altered practical behavior. It can lie within the *intention* of the legal regulations to give a nudge to that possible development, but it would be absurd if the law-making subject wanted to run that process: because whether the possible development becomes real is not left in the hands of that subject.[317] This is not to deny that there can be a duty to give the nudge that can push in such a direction.

The ethical quality of a person does not depend on the person alone—neither the ability to grasp values nor the way the person is filled with them is a matter of her liberty. Nevertheless the ethical duty (the simple fact of what should be done) addresses itself to her liberty and makes sense only in reference to that. If it's not left in our hands to procure ourselves access to values,

---

316. [*Habitus* is Latin for "disposition" or "customary comportment." Its meaning is close to that of the German *Verhalt.* The term for "morality" introduced here is *Moral,* in contrast to the usual term *Sittlichkeit.* In the present context, "morality" refers to what people in a given time and place happen to believe about right and wrong.]

317. [An example may be drawn from the history of race relations in the United States. Before the middle of the twentieth century, "morality" as commonly accepted included the practices of racial segregation in education, employment, and most sectors of public life. After civil rights legislation was enacted, social practices were forced to change by law. In the wake of those legal changes, the inner attitudes of individuals also began to change, and the values of society as a whole gradually shifted. By the end of the twentieth century, racial segregation and discrimination had come to be considered immoral. The process of transformation of "morality" continues in this area.]

we're still free to "listen" for them, and that can be required. If it remains without result, then a disvalue may well attach to that, but it is not a violation of duty.

b) The state in its relation to ethical norms

Since the state is to be seen as a subject of free acts, ethical duties can—apparently—be imposed on the state. Yet it is clear from the start that the state is not an ethical subject in the same sense as it is a legal subject. To be a state *means* to be law's subject.[318] In the instant when it ceases to bear the responsibility for the operative legal system, the state ceases to exist. It does not cease to exist if it is living unconcerned by ethical norms, even though it should pertain to a state that it is affected by them. The manner in which the ethical norms impinge upon the state is one more particular problem. In order to apprehend the just-so of "good" or the just-so of "should" in any particular instance,[319] it is required that cognizance can be taken of the underlying value. Cognizance of values is taken in acts of feeling. The state as such is incapable of taking cognizance of anything at all, and in particular is incapable of feeling. Its sole domain is the execution of free acts, which includes getting things done (understood as realization of a state of affairs).

A positive or a negative ethical value can attach to those acts, in accordance with that which is realized through them. And in that sense, depending upon how morally relevant or indifferent they are, they can be designated as "mandatory," as "forbidden," or as "allowed." However, the state is not capable of discerning which acts "should be" and which "should not be." That can be

---

318. [*Rechtssubjekt,* "law's subject," connotes the activity of making law. The state is the subject that does the law-making.]

319. [Phenomenological terms are used here that have no English equivalent. *Zur Erfassung eines Wert- bzw. Sollensverhalts* is literally: "To the apprehension of a value- or, respectively, of a should-holding."]

done only by the persons whom the state uses as its agents.

Now, the question is whether the "should" is only focused on them as individual persons, or also focused on them as representatives of the state; and correlatively, whether only duties of persons (or groups of persons, as the case may be) can be spoken of, but not moral duties of states. Surely it makes no sense to say that the agents of the state are feeling in its place, the same way they make regulations or do other things in its place.[320] For we saw that the proxy power extends only to that which in principle lies within the realm of the "can-do." This does not prevent ethical demands from availing themselves, so to speak, of the agents—and generally of all individual persons who have anything to do with the state—in order to be able to penetrate through them to the state.[321] For one thing, the persons have the responsibility on their own, to refuse certain actions of the state and on the other hand to execute others. But beyond that, they make it possible to speak of a certain impingement upon the state by ethical demands. Not, surely, so that it would be commensurate with its sense as state to do or to omit something because it is a duty.

The state is no more a person, in the full sense of the word, than it is a moral being. To the persons who stand in the service of the state, and to all those with whom its existence is bound up, *their* duties are made perceptible, including those which result from their relation to the state. But beyond that, they can help bring it about that the actions of the state with moral relevance become open to criticism at their root, and not for the first time in their effect, meaning that the state itself initiates what is right and forgoes what is not right. That is possible only when moral motives have such power in the persons within its sovereign territory that they refuse their recognition to the state that does not take those motives into account. Then it is necessary to the self-preservation of the state, and therefore commensurate with its

---

320. [Literally, "as they do or determine in its place."]

321. [This sentence is obscure in German as well.]

sense, that the state remain in agreement with the moral law.[322]

Now let's move on to the question of *what* can be demanded of the state in the name of ethics in this indirect way. To put it very generally: a particular content of the laws it makes. To the extent lying within the realm of possibility, the state *should* realize values, or cooperate in the realization of values. The first value to consider, a value whose realization is specially assigned to the state, is that of justice. In this sense, it is to be demanded of the state that its law be "right law." After that [comes] the value whose real carrier is not the state itself *qua* state, but rather the community embraced by the state.[323] The state can be of service for "personality development" through institutions that it creates, or even through the fact that it leaves certain areas free from state control and relies upon the initiative of individuals or private groups. In that case, the requisite content of the legal regulations is a self-limitation of the civil authority.

Among the values whose carrier can be the community organized into a state are the personal *moral* values (which indeed are not the unique personal values).[324] The task of making a moral

---

322. From this is produced a rule for practical policy, for example, the politics of parties that would like to fashion the state into a "moral realm": that they must set about their work with the *people* and not with the *state*. The state for its part must accommodate itself to the ethos of the people. On the other hand, reforming the state according to fundamental moral principles *without* such a basis [in the ethos of the people] is preposterous and inimical to the sense of state *(sinnwidrig und staatsfeindlich)*.

323. [*Qua* is Latin for "as far as," hence "insofar as the state is a state." The value that comes second in rank after justice is community. The sentence is ambiguous but supports the following translation: "After that is community, the value whose real carrier is not the state itself *qua* state, but which rather is embraced in the state." *(Sodann der Wert, dessen eigentlicher Träger nicht er selbst qua Staat, sondern die in ihm zusammengefaßt Gemeinschaft ist.)*]

324. [*Die einzigen Personwerte,* "the unique personal values," refers to the unique value that each person is, as opposed to whatever

community out of the community that is its sovereign sector (*scilicet*[325] insofar as it lies within its power) can make it a duty for the state to combat the prevailing morality through its legal regulations and to give them ethical norms as content.

Finally, the "duties" of the state involve not only its behavior toward the community that coincides with it as well as toward the persons and groups belonging to it, but also its behavior toward other states and non-governmental organizations. And here the possibility of a conflict of values is heightened even more than with the claims mentioned before, which indeed could already require something contradictory from the state. It's not hard to realize that fraud, robbery, and any intervention into the sphere of interest of another arising out of pure covetousness is to be rejected in the transactions of states just as among discrete persons.

It's different when the life of two states and their possibility of development are not compatible with one another. Then you've got a real conflict of duties: values are opposed to one another, and one of them is to be actualized only at the expense of the other. The conflict would resolve itself if the situation were such that each state were burdened only with the duty of caring for itself and for the individuals belonging to it. An external test of power would take the place of the ethical conflict. Neither of the participants would have any question about which value it should realize, but only about whether it succeeds in breaking through the obstacles that stand in the way of the fulfillment of its duty, which itself is clear.

That view, however, doubtless does not fit the situation. It is never ethically permissible, when faced with a value that will be affected by an intended transaction, to close your eyes and leave it entirely out of consideration. Where values enter into competition, you always get a conflict that must come to settlement inside of every single participating person, and cannot be resolved by an

---

distinctive set of values each may happen to choose. Any person as such is a unique value, in Stein's estimation.]

325. [*Scilicet* is Latin for "that is to say."]

external struggle among several persons.[326] If any person decides the question in practice as though one of the conflicting values "didn't matter" and would not need to be taken into consideration at all by her, then a disvalue attaches to that behavior, even if the person is led to the same decision that would turn out to be the morally right one with reference to the value left out of consideration.

Thus it is a duty of the state, or of those who represent it, to keep in view not only those values for which the state is the carrier and appointed guardian, but also the others that are involved in its behavior. That says nothing about what the state has to decide in the individual case. Actually, in the great majority of cases that come under consideration, it will happen that the decision-makers lack the ability for an adequate apprehension and assessment of the values in question.[327] And similarly, the adjudication of whether the decision in question was correct exceeds human telling. If the different participants decide differently—and even with conscientious ethical deliberation, that's the only way for any external struggle to come about—then in that's an index that the decision was a wrong one anyway, at least on one side.

As our reflections showed, in all these cases it's to be understood very much *cum grano salis* that the *state* would get into a conflict or would have to make ethical decisions.[328] Everything transpires within the individuals. It becomes significant for the stance that ascribes to the state its own proper sense, but only as one factor that the state has to reckon with. The theory

---

326. [This apparently non-violent stance is undercut by Stein's argument for the necessity of armed forces. See above, pp. 134-6.]

327. [Literally, "that the adequate conception and assessment of the values standing in question exceeds the ability of those upon whom the decision devolves."]

328. [*Cum grano salis* is Latin for "with a grain of salt." Although in a manner of speaking we attribute ethical conflicts and decisions to the state, this is not literally true.]

of the state in [the philosophy of] German Idealism considered the state as the implement for bringing the moral law into dominance in the world. According to Fichte, freedom is the instrument that makes possible the realization of the moral idea in life.[329] It divides into internal and external freedom (which means protection against the freedom of others), and this is safeguarded by the legal system in the state. So just legislation is to be claimed as a prerequisite of morality.[330]

Against this argumentation, various misgivings arise.[331] For one thing, freedom (strictly speaking) is to be restricted by nothing. Coercive measures—as one might apply them against the others by virtue of his freedom—have only the sense of motives that try to push the person in a certain direction; we established this earlier.[332] Whether the person goes in that direction is something that always remains her own affair. There might be persons who mostly let themselves drift and make no use of their freedom. Nevertheless they remain in possession of their freedom

---

329. [Johann Gottlieb Fichte (1762-1814) interpreted and developed the thought of Immanuel Kant. His publications are extensive, and Stein gives no specific citation. Relevant passages may be found in: "The Closed Commercial State," *The Political Thought of the German Romantics, 1793-1815,* 86-102, trans. H.S. Reiss and P. Brown (Oxford: Blackwell, 1955); *The Vocation of Man,* trans. Peter Preuss (Indianapolis: Hackett Publishing Company, 1987); "The System of Ethics According to the Principles of Philosophy," *The Educational Theory of J.G. Fichte,* 126-133, trans. George H. Turnbull (London, Hodder and Stoughton, 1926).]

330. [*Rechtsgesetz,* "just legislation," could also mean something like "enacting just laws."]

331. The critique of Fichte's conception of the moral vocation of the state that is mounted here does not extend to the entire "theory of the state," which contains in addition some excellent comments about the fabric of the state.

332. [See above, Part I, §2, section c (toward the end) and section l. See also note 199. The term "motive" has a technical meaning in phenomenology and contrasts with "cause."]

and can fall back upon it at any time. Therefore the law comes into question as a prerequisite of morality at most *as a matter of fact*, to the extent that the law may clear away impediments that stand in the way of moral motives. The law is not a *conditio sine qua non*.[333] Secondly, according to our findings we've got no business claiming that the law is merely a prerequisite of morality. The law has its *own proper* substantial meaning. Furthermore, only by virtue of that substantial meaning is the law able to intervene motivatingly in the moral life (as punishment can prompt repentance).

These misgivings in principle do not rule out the possibility that in fact the state may be able, through its legal measures, to educate for morality—since motives are surely of very great significance for the formation of will and of character—and to facilitate education for morality even for the other powers. It may be that the "world plan" avails itself of the state in order to achieve this purpose. But this is not prescribed as necessary in the state's own proper fabric.[334]

§5. The state as carrier of historic process

Another issue emerges in connection with the last one. The state—according to Fichte and Hegel—is the proper instrument of morality and freedom, and so is *the carrier of historical process*.[335] For the content of history for them subsists precisely

---

333. [*Conditio sine qua non* is Latin for "condition without which not," or necessary condition. Morality does not require laws.]

334. [In the last two sentences, the word "state" is supplied for the pronoun *seiner*, although the meaning is ambiguous. The term "world plan" may be an allusion to Hegel's view of history; see below.]

335. [Literally, "In its property as instrument of morality and freedom, the state is—according to Fichte and Hegel—the carrier of historical occurrence." Georg Wilhelm Friedrich Hegel (1770-1831) was a younger contemporary of Fichte. Both philosophers made

in the development of the moral idea. That conception is not refuted as long as we cannot recognize in principle that it is the sense of the state to protect the freedom of individuals, much less that the freedom of individuals is transferred to the state.

The first issue would be what stance we should take toward such a determination of the content of history. It is certainly correct to consider history as a process of spiritual development.[336] But what is developing there cannot be "freedom." For freedom, in the strict sense to which we have pegged the term, is not something that can unfold itself or develop. It can only be there or not be there. And in individual cases, there can be a moment in which freedom starts to be. Only in a non-literal sense can you talk about any development of freedom; namely, to the extent that it is possible for freedom progressively to gain control over mere compulsion.[337] For what develops is not freedom but its carrier: the individual person or the community of persons. Hegel is going in this direction when he talks about the mind's development toward the consciousness of its freedom. This is a purely formal element: that "mind" as such should take charge of itself or that the person should do so. We set aside for now the question

---

important contributions to German Idealism, and their work would have to be addressed in any serious philosophical discussion of history. Hegel used the term "phenomenology" with a different meaning than that later adopted by Husserl and Stein.]

336. [*Geistigen Entfaltungsprozeß*, "process of spiritual development," is literally "mental process of development." *Geistig* can mean mental, intellectual, or spiritual, according to the context. Hegel used the term *Geist* to mean an impersonal Mind that comes to know itself in human history. He held that "the history of the world is none other than the progress of the consciousness of freedom"; see the introduction to *The Philosophy of History*, trans. J. Sibree (New York: Dover Publications, 1956). This Hegelian notion of Mind is the background of Stein's comments here.]

337. [*Bloßen Getriebenwerden*, "mere compulsion," is literally "simply being impelled."]

whether this element suffices for determining the content of history.[338]

In any case, in order to get from there to the inclusion of the state, you need a middle step, which is found in Fichte: that the awakening of the individual to freedom is possible only in the community, not for isolated human beings. Once again, inspection does not disclose even this as a necessity in principle.[339] All that is necessary, in order for each individual to arrive at the possession of his freedom, is a sense of himself.[340] Freedom is within him and needs only to be grasped. Why this should be possible only with regard to free persons, and not perhaps in connection with inanimate matter, is something that's not to be rationally comprehended, even though it is factually so without a doubt. Thus the community would be necessary so that the individual could awaken to freedom. But the state would be necessary so that this possibility would become a reality and so that intimidation by other individuals would not hinder someone in the use of his freedom.

We don't want to dispute the fact that such a connection [between freedom and the state] actually obtains. Yet we cannot concede that that's all there is to the content of history, the

---

338. [Literally, "Whether this purely formal element, that 'the mind' absolutely (*schlechthin*) or that the person should take itself in hand, suffices for the determination of the content of history, this we leave aside temporarily."]

339. [Literally, "Again, this also is not to be seen into (*einzusehen*) as a necessity in principle." A phenomenologist studies essences by "seeing into" them to discern what is required to make them what they are. Stein uses technical vocabulary to indicate that community is not an essential component of freedom, even though it is a practical requirement for the realization of freedom.]

340. [*Besinnung auf sich selbst,* "sense of himself," could also mean "self-consciousness." *Besinnung* is not the usual phenomenological term for consciousness.]

"purpose" of the state and its significance for history.[341] What's needed here, as a connecting step [in the argument], is a closer examination of what is to be understood by "moral idea." In no way is this term synonymous with freedom. Free decision is morally relevant, to be sure, but not yet characterized as positively or negatively valued. Yet that polarity pertains to moral value, just as it does to any value. Decision about it does not depend upon freedom, but upon the motives on which the decision is based, and on *what* is grasped with freedom: whether that itself is worthwhile or not.

So, precisely when you put history together with the "moral idea," you have to bring in *concrete values*. Therefore, development toward morality would not mean just awakening to freedom, but training of susceptibility for values of all kinds and progressing in the exercise of freedom toward the realization of values. Therefore the content of history turns out to be the creation of culture.[342] You get the same result if you take a look at the flow of history itself and don't start from any recollected point in time. And no such point in time can be significant for a historical-philosophical consideration at all, except to the extent that it corresponds with a tendency that has been detected for historical occurrence.

If we conceptualize history as the course of mental life in which "cultures" develop, then the connections among history, community, and state appear in a new light. If we think back to the earlier discussions of the ethnic group as a "culturally creative personality" and its desire for organization as a state, then individualistically oriented speculation about the purpose of the

---

341. [Literally, "that with this the content of history, the 'purpose' of the state and its significance for history would be circumscribed."]

342. In support of this, see Emil Lask, *Fichtes Idealismus und die Geschichte* (Tübingen: Mohr, 1914) 4: "The rational operation of the species . . . that is, the quintessence of that which rises out of it as absolutely valuable, is *culture,* the culture in its development *history*."

state and the content of history falls apart. What role the individual plays in history, and conversely what significance history has
for the individual—those are further questions that we must defer
here. For one thing, the assumption that you have to start with the
individual in order to comprehend the sense of history is to be
rejected as a prejudice.[343]

The disclosure of the connection of state and culture invali-
dates the struggle for precedence between political and cultural
history which has occupied the historians in the last decades. A
historiography that disregards the unfolding of culture is no more
viable than one that ignores states. It's understandable and even
defensible for state-related matters to take a certain precedence in
the practical business of history, because not only are states
historical formations alongside others but at the same they are the
landmarks that make it possible for any one historic feature to be
isolated in the midst of the whole multiplicity of others.[344]
Because states are centers by means of which a field becomes
definitely outlined and graspable (and understood, surely, as a
mental sphere, not only as land), that's the data to start with if you
want to survey the flow of mental events—even episodically.[345]

---

343. [Literally: "it is to be rejected as a prejudice that the sense
of history must be conceived from the individual on out."]

344. [Literally, "the points of orientation that make it possible
for one (historical appearance) to find itself throughout (*sich
hindurchzufinden*) through the whole multiplicity of historic appearances." In phenomenology, eidetic analysis cannot begin until "one"
of something is grasped; that is, until discrete unities are constituted
out of the chaotic multiplicity of appearances. Stein indicates that a
state is a relatively easy thing to isolate and name. With that done,
then other phenomena can coalesce into their own proper unities
around it. Stein's remarks apply to history-writing, as a constructive
project of understanding; she is not talking about real-world events
taken naively and without adverting to their constructed character.]

345. [*Geistig,* "mental" in both places can also mean "spiritual"
or even "cultural." *Geist* in the vocabulary of German Idealism is
ordinarily translated "Mind," and this is the context here.]

That's why the rise and fall of a state and every segment of its evolution are at the same time indices for epochs in cultural life. If a new state arises, either it's an indication that a self-contained cultural area has given itself its external form and then is pointing backwards to the cultural development that has produced this outcome, or else the new state gives notice of the fruit that this event will bear for further development. Or it indicates the splintering of a heretofore unified cultural area or perhaps the welding together of different cultural areas—then you've got to track down the development that made such an interface possible, and the influences that emanate from this interface [of different cultures]. Any historical presentation that disregarded these connections, and contented itself with the events of state formation purely as such, would have only the significance of a cornerstone and could not claim the value of a "conclusive" achievement, that is, of an achievement such that, at least according to the idea, it had gathered into one point the sense of the historical occurrence.

Let's go back now to the question of the historic importance of the state. Neither by contemplating historic occurrence as such, nor by contemplating the state, can you arrive at the insight that the state should be conceived of as an instrument for bringing about an ultimate purpose of history.[346] According to its idea the state has nothing to do with history. That means, being a historic

---

346. [Literally, "can it be made insightful that the state would be to be conceived as an instrument to the bringing about of an ultimate goal of history." In the technical language of phenomenology, to entertain a concept with insight means to see its essence clearly and with certainty. Its essence is its "idea"—a term that recalls the Greek philosophical lexicon, where *eidos* is "that which is seen" and where the present tense of the verb "to know" is identical with the perfect tense of the verb *idein,* "to see." Eidetic analysis in phenomenology is idea-analysis, usually rendered in English as analysis of essences, as they appear with insight. Stein is arguing against the assertion that the state's essence is to bring about the ultimate goal of history. That goal, according to Hegel, was the self-realization of freedom for Mind; see above.]

agent does not belong to the idea of the state. You can conceive of a state detached from all references to the historical context. On the other hand, history does not depend in principle upon the state. You can conceive of historic events in which a state would play no role and which would be carried only by individuals and communities without state organization.

This detachability in principle doesn't alter the fact that the state[347] is very well suited, on the basis of what it is according to its idea, for being a carrier of historic events: by being free to submit all mental life to its guidance, it relates to everything that is historically relevant and secures meaning for everything. And so, factually, it is of such importance in history that—as we argued earlier—you can most easily become a master in the academic treatment of history if you deal with it as history of states. On the other hand the empirical states, according to their factual arising, are historic patterns evolving out of the flow of history in the making; this must be maintained. They stay in that flow and emerge as centers of operation.

It is as such an operative center that the state makes possible on a broad scale that which we have designated the sense of history: the realization of values. But—as already argued—the state is only able to achieve this thanks to its ontic fabric. That the state must do it is not included as necessary in that fabric.

§6. State and religion

There's another problem that we have to take a look at from this angle, which we haven't touched upon up to now: the relation of the state and the religious sphere. By all appearances, the absolute precedence of the religious sphere before all others, and the absolute obedience to God's commandments required by that, are incompatible with the unconditional obedience that the state

---

347. Here and in the following remarks, "the state" doesn't mean the idea of the state, but rather "everything that is a state." [Stein indicates that the eidetic analysis ceases at this point. Empirical consideration of concretely existing states now begins.]

claims for its ordinances. First and foremost, every human being stands under the supreme sovereign, and no earthly relation of sovereignty can change anything about that. If the believer receives a command from God—be it immediately in prayer or be it by the mediation of God's representative on earth—then he must obey, whether or not he defies the will of the state in doing so.[348] Here we confront two claims to sovereignty that mutually exclude each other in their absoluteness.

Therefore it's entirely understandable if the state treats the individual believer, but above all the church—the visible and permanent embodiment of that sovereign claim breaking through the state's sovereignty—with distrust and occasionally with open hostility. Conversely you can understand that among believers the conception of the state as an Antichrist would emerge again and again.

There is no solution in principle for the conflict arising from the properties of the of civil and religious spheres. Only a factual compromise is possible.[349] On one hand, a compromise is produced through the word of the Lord: Render unto Caesar that which is Caesar's. This indicates that the state and obedience with regard to it are willed by God or at least permitted by God.

---

348. [Although the last three sentences seem to affirm the priority of divine authority, they are qualified by the phrase, "by all appearances" *(allem Anschein nach)*. Stein is setting up an argument by stating one side of it plainly. In this context, the claim of divine authority is described but not endorsed. The resolution which Stein herself endorses comes later.]

349. [*Ein faktischer Ausgleich,* "a factual compromise," must be worked out on a case by case basis, empirically, since an *eidetic* analysis of the respective essences of church and state does not support the primacy of either. The same solution is attributed to Jesus of Nazareth by the synoptic gospels; see Mark 12:17 and parallels. Although Stein cites that solution explicitly, this need not indicate that she has read the gospels at this point in her career. The allusion is a well known literary one. Nevertheless, here is the first instance where Stein calls Jesus Lord in print.]

However it's only a conditional recognition of state sovereignty
—state sovereignty presupposes that the state does not prevent
giving God what is God's. If the state adopts this in the regulation
of its life *of its own accord*, then you've got the basis for a
factually frictionless coexistence of the sovereign state and the
religious sphere, or the church.[350]

This compromise is conceivable in various concrete modes.
The most relevant one to examine here is the mode designated as
theocracy. In a theocratically ordered political system, the
conception of the faithful considers the civil order as a divine
institution. If a people lives its whole life in the face of God, if
they anxiously try to let his will lead them at every step, and
believe that for them that will is known through the mouth of their
priests—then it's only self-evident that that ethnic group also
seeks to set up their state according to the instructions of divine
revelation, and either recognizes the priests as outright possessors
of civil authority or grants to them in some mode or other a share
in the guidance of the state.

This in no way sets the state above any other mode of living.
Marriage and family life, relations with the hired help, with living
and nonliving possessions, concern for the satisfaction of
primitive appetites of life—all of that is covered by divine law.
There can be no question of a preeminent place for the state
except in the sense that the divine Sovereign of the world might
be using the state as an instrument by means of which he might be
managing the communities embraced within the state and the
individuals belonging to them. Hardly anyone would concede, on

---

350. [The original German text does not imply that the religious
sphere is equivalent to the church, excluding the synagogue and other
non-Christian religious institutions. "Or" translates the abbreviation
bzw., which could also be translated "and accordingly" or even "or
. . . as the case may be." This abbreviation stands for *beziehungs-
weise* and merely asserts that what was said about the first term
(religious sphere) also applies to the second term (church). The
church is an instance of something found in the religious sphere.]

that basis alone, that the modality of state still would be maintained in this case. Obviously, this apparatus would not be governed by itself at all, but by an external power.

Yet that way of conceptualizing it does not do justice to the situation.[351] In that God chooses himself a people as his sovereign sphere and endows that people with state-type organization, he founds a state whose will is not different from his own. You could say that in that state, he himself would be presiding over the government. Admittedly, not like an earthly sovereign, who represents the state and implements its intentions. Rather, the state itself must be thought of in such a way that its acts, depending upon divine commands, still always stand in harmony with the divine will. God gives—in the sense of this conceptualization—to his chosen people a state that commands and regulates in his spirit, so that the representatives of the state are at the same time to be regarded as executors of the divine will. If fulfillment of the divine will is what makes the state's existence possible, then that prescribes for the state its proper sense: to bring its statutes and its actions into accord with those commandments. Then divine dominion and the sovereignty of the state do not stand in contradiction to one another.[352]

We've described theocracy as *one possible* modality of state. But doesn't the idea of the divine governance of the world call for *every* state to be conceived of in this way? Doesn't this idea force us to look upon every earthly possessor of any civil authority merely as a placeholder of the supreme Sovereign? Were it so, then still it would always remain merely a *fact,* and the idea of the

---

351. [Stein continues to describe the idea of theocracy, as understood by the faithful. This is eidetic analysis, not empirical historical description. She does not mean to assert that such a state has in fact been established by God at any point in human history.]

352. [Stein argues that the idea of theocracy involves no necessary contradictions. This argument stops short of saying that God has in fact founded such a state so that a theocracy has actually existed somewhere.]

state is not tied to facts.[353] It would be rendered conceivable only [by deduction] from the idea of divine governance of the world, not from the fabric of the state. Because if nothing in the world can happen without the divine *placet,*[354] then any worldly sovereignty independent of him is also inconceivable. With that, we would arrive at the astounding result that the state, which according to its idea seems to have its existence threatened by the religious sphere, in reality can't even exist unless sustained by that sphere.[355]

Conversely, and in the same vein, nothing is to be deduced from the idea of theocracy about what mode the states would have to have, or whether only *one* possessor of the civil authority or several would be possible, or how to plan the distribution of their functions. On the contrary, [reasoning deductively] from precisely the standpoint just indicated, you would have to accept as divinely willed any empirical modality of state that came along.[356]

---

353. [The "it" in "were it so" (and in the next sentence as well) refers to the hypothetical situation mentioned in the last sentence: a situation in which any earthly civil authority is just a placeholder for the supreme sovereign, presumably God. Such a situation may or may not be actualized. If actualized, it is a fact; but it is *merely* a fact, since this actualization is not a *necessary* implication following from *either* the idea of divine governance of the universe, *or* the idea of the state. Both of those ideas are essential concepts; they are not "facts" because they are not items to be found in the world considered in the natural attitude, phenomenologically speaking. Compare the conversation between Jesus and Pilate, John 18:33-19:11.]

354. [*Placet* is Latin for "it pleases." The term indicates approval or permission, not necessarily pleasure.]

355. [Literally, "in reality can exist precisely only sustained by that sphere."]

356. [Theocracy, understood now as the idea of divine governance of the world, implies that any kind of state at all that comes into existence must necessarily have done so with divine permission. Any state that exists must be sanctioned by God.]

On the other hand, if you assume that the system of earthly states subsists in its own right (which likewise would be something to be shown only as a fact and not as a necessity), then you get the possibility of a discrepancy between God's commandment and the state's, which doesn't come up at all with the other way of conceiving it, and new problems arise with respect to the possible connections between the two. First—just as in every other sphere of value—for the individual it presents the possibility of a conflict between what the state demands from him and what holds for him as the will of God. Suppose an individual gets himself into such a conflict, and he decides—doubtless in accord with the ranking of the values—in the sense of his religious conviction. Then he's acting as an enemy of the state: in that he refuses the precept of the state, he undermines its existence.

And there's the question of what stance the state should take toward this. There are various viewpoints to consider here. Generally speaking, it can be designated a precept of prudence not to prescribe something for citizens if there are strong motives within them that rebel against it. According to what was set forth earlier, the existence of the state depends upon whether its "regulations" are followed. So the state as far as possible must avoid giving those regulations any content that is designed to excite vehement opposition. Obviously there are limits to this self-restraint. The vital interests of the state could render it precisely necessary for the state to have to place the most severe strictures upon its citizens. In such a dilemma, where the state's existence is threatened from both directions, it all comes down to an assessment of where the greater danger probably lies, and ultimately to a test whether the state can get by either with the strictures or without them. Apart from such cases, however, heads of state themselves are behaving as enemies of the state if, through the content of their regulations, they alienate the powers that they were supposed to ally with—the impulses in the souls of individuals.[357]

---

357. [Literally, "if through the content of their regulations they make into enemies the powers that they were supposed to make into

What about the behavior of the state toward a citizen who refuses obedience to it on religious grounds? Apart from that precept of prudence, one possible criterion to consider is whether or not the representatives of the state would be able to recognize the conflict as justifiable in itself. If the responsible persons, with a sympathetic examination of the crucial motives, arrive at the result that it's a matter of an error of religious sentiment, then you could think that they would have the right to uphold their command regardless of the sentiment. Yet that would not be the right solution (even apart from the prudential rule, which indeed obtains entirely independently from the justifiability of the motives at hand). Or at most [it might be right] in an altogether particular exigency.

The problem before which we now stand is a purely ethical one, and it admits of being cast in a general form. With respect to the behavior of a person, does even an *intended* value merit consideration, if that value seems to be threatened by this behavior? In order to find the right answer, it must be made clear that values truly obtaining, or disvalues as the case may be, could be connected with that intended value. A disvalue attaches to the decision in favor of a lesser value every time, even when the value that is being sacrificed for it is only *intentionally* higher. And when someone is tempted to such a negative-valued decision by the state's coercive authority, then the exercise of the state's coercive authority is also to be regarded as negative-valued.

In no way is it said, incidentally, that it always must be decided in the sense of this perspective.[358] Conversely, in the case

---

allies for themselves—the soul-ish *(seelisch)* impulses of individuals." In English there is no adjective corresponding to the noun "soul." The context is not necessary religious.]

358. [Stein argues that such an exercise of coercive authority is wrong even if it does not succeed, that is, even if the person experiencing the coercion resists it and refrains from deciding against her own intended values.]

of conflict it can become necessary to set aside this perspective. What is generally required is only that it be taken into consideration along with ethical deliberations. Undoubtedly, the behavior of the state would be ethically beyond reproach if it succeeded in dissolving the aforementioned value illusion and therefore in bringing a solution to the conflict within the heart of the individual. If the state is incapable of doing that, then one possible way out is to dispense those individuals in whom such motives are present from the fulfillment of the commands in question.

Such a dispensation is one of those self-limitations of the state that have been mentioned several times: a violation of sovereignty through disobedience of the citizens is prevented by it. In any event, if the number of those self-limitations of the civil authority grows to the point where the state can no longer achieve what is required for its maintenance, then they amount to a self-dissolution. Whether that is a duty is something that cannot be decided generally, but only case by case. In any event it will be possible to say: any state in which there is such a chasm between the government and the governed that the latter regard all demands placed upon them in the interest of the state as an imposition whose fulfillment they cannot reconcile with their conscience—any such state would already have lost the basis of its existence, and no coercive authority could put it back again.

But what if it's not a matter of a [merely] intended value, but rather of a value truly subsisting or one that not even the civil authority doubts? Then obviously you're no longer facing the issue of protecting lone citizens from a conflict by dispensing them from a command. Rather, it's the issue of whether the state is allowed to enact a precept that clashes with religious values recognized by the state itself (that is, by its representatives). A civil statute that would restrict liturgical services or hamper the clergy in the activities of pastoral care undoubtedly would be reprehensible, and the state that would enact it would be disfigured with a scar.

And this demand for consideration of religious values by the state remains in force even if it seems to jeopardize vital interests of the state. Just as an individual in such a case has nothing left to do but place his life in God's hand, neither can it be conceded to the state as a moral right to hold its own in the struggle against religious values. (Nothing about this is changed by the fact that the state itself, according to its own proper sense, has no relation to the religious sphere, and the ethical conflict as such is played out within the soul of its representative.)

So far we've been thinking about only the possibility of a disruptive intervention of the state in religious life. Let's inquire beyond that into whether it can be designated as the state's duty positively to foster religious life. The possibilities for such a positive fostering are rather limited. For religious life transpires in a sphere in which nothing can be brought about and nothing can be undone through legislation or through arbitrary initiatives in general. However, legislation, while not being productive itself, can free up productive powers or can inhibit their deployment. If you set up institutions that disclose to certain individuals for the first time the possibility of coming into contact with the religious sphere, you create "opportunities" for the kindling of new religious life, which is something that you don't control. Provided that the state is in a position to provide such a service, it can be proposed to the state through its agencies in the manner described earlier. The value that attaches to this ancillary efficacy is a mediated one.

The question of whether the state can be a carrier of its own religious values is to be answered negatively, according to the preceding investigations. For religious values belong to a personal sphere, which the state lacks. The state has no soul, for one thing, as we already stated earlier. An additional reason, of course, is that the state is not anchored in the soul of the persons who belong to it.

Make no mistake about this. There's an allegiance to the state that is an affair of the soul. And so are all the other motives that impel individuals to "recognize" the state or to refuse it. But those motives form only the groundwork upon which the existence of the state relies, as was repeatedly stressed. They have nothing to do with what the state as such is.[359] For that lies totally within the sphere of freedom. The person plays a role in this only *qua* free subject and not *qua* ensouled being.[360] Therefore the individual who is living in the state can be holy or profane, and so can the ethnic community whose life it regulates; but the state itself cannot.

---

359. [Literally, "they are indifferent for that which the state as such is."]

360. [*Seelisches Wesen,* "ensouled being," is literally "soul-ish entity." *Wesen* can also mean "essence" in phenomenology. The Latin term *qua* indicates what aspect of the person it is that enables the person to play this role. Stein says that although the motive that urges toward pledging allegiance to the state is felt in the soul, yet it won't be the soul as such that makes the decision to embrace that motive and commit to supporting the state. It takes a free subject to do this. Stein does not assign freedom or powers of decision and action to the soul at this point in her philosophical career.]

Index

The Institute of Carmelite Studies promotes research and publication in the field of Carmelite spirituality. Its members are Discalced Carmelites, part of a Roman Catholic community—friars, nuns, and laity—who are heirs to the teaching and way of life of Teresa of Jesus and John of the Cross, men and women dedicated to contemplation and to ministry in the Church and the world. Information concerning their way of life is available through local diocesan Vocation Offices or from the Vocation Directors' Offices:

5345 University Avenue, Chicago IL 60615

PO Box 3420, San Jose, CA 95156-3420

5151 Marylake Drive, Little Rock, AR 72206